Test Bank
to accompany

Introduction to Teaching
Becoming a Professional

Second Edition

Don Kauchak
University of Utah

Paul Eggen
University of Northern Florida

PEARSON
Merrill
Prentice Hall

Upper Saddle River, New Jersey
Columbus, Ohio

Copyright © 2005 by Pearson Education, Inc., Upper Saddle River, New Jersey 07458.
Pearson Prentice Hall. All rights reserved. Printed in the United States of America. This publication is protected by Copyright and permission should be obtained from the publisher prior to any prohibited reproduction, storage in a retrieval system, or transmission in any form or by any means, electronic, mechanical, photocopying, recording, or likewise. For information regarding permission(s), write to: Rights and Permissions Department.

Pearson Prentice Hall™ is a trademark of Pearson Education, Inc.
Pearson® is a registered trademark of Pearson plc
Prentice Hall® is a registered trademark of Pearson Education, Inc.
Merrill® is a registered trademark of Pearson Education, Inc.

Instructors of classes using Kauchak & Eggen, *Introduction to Education: Becoming a Professional, Second Edition,* may reproduce material from the test bank for classroom use.

10 9 8 7 6 5 4 3 2

ISBN: 0-13-142820-9

This Test Item File is just one part of Prentice Hall's comprehensive testing support service, which also includes TestGen for Windows and Macintosh.

TestGen: What is it?

TestGen is a test generator program that lets you view and edit test bank questions, transfer them to tests, and then administer those tests on paper, on a local area network, or over the Web. The program provides many options for organizing and displaying test banks and tests. A built-in random number and text generator makes it ideal for creating multiple versions of questions and tests. Powerful search and sort functions let you easily locate questions and arrange them in the order you prefer.

TestGen makes test creation easy and convenient with uncluttered side-by-side test bank and test windows, symbol palettes, expression templates, keyboard shortcuts, a graphing tool, variable text and numbers, and graphics. In addition, you can assign multiple descriptors to any question, including page references, topic, skill, objective, difficulty level, and answer explanations.

TestGen provides several options for online testing—a simple export to WebCT and BlackBoard formats, a conversion to HTML files, as well as a TestGen plug-in that displays the test in a Web browser and reports student results to the gradebook of Pearson's CourseCompass course management system.

TestGen: How do I get it?

The TestGen software is free. To order a test bank for a specific TestGen title, you may contact your local representative or call our Faculty Support Services Department at 1-800-526-0485. Please identify the main text author and title.

Toll-free **technical support** is offered to users of TestGen at 1-800-677-6337 or via e-mail at media.support@pearsoned.com.

TABLE OF CONTENTS

CHAPTER ONE

WHY BECOME A TEACHER?

Knowledge-Level Items

1. According to surveys conducted by the National Education Association, which of the following are the two most important reasons people give for choosing to teach?
    a. Short working hours and long summer vacations
    b. Long summer vacations and autonomy
    c. Autonomy and professional status
    d. Working with young people and contributing to society

2. You're a seventh-grade English teacher in your second year of teaching. Of the following the best example of an intrinsic reward for you is likely to be
    a. a salary supplement for sponsoring the school yearbook.
    b. a former student coming back to visit you.
    c. a 2-week winter holiday vacation.
    d. tenure after your third year of teaching.

3. You're an eighth-grade math teacher. Of the following the best example of an intellectual reward in teaching is likely to be
    a. a high school senior coming back to visit you.
    b. seeing students successfully predict the next number in the sequence 1, 1, 2, 3, 5, 8 . . . .
    c. having one of your students come up to you and say, "I used to hate math, but now I really like it."
    d. receiving a salary supplement for sponsoring the school's math club.

4. You're a third-grade teacher. Of the following the best example of an extrinsic reward is likely to be
    a. a parent calling and thanking you for the extra help you've given her daughter.
    b. receiving a salary supplement for being the grade chairperson for third grade in your school.
    c. seeing Melissa, one of your low-achieving students, improve dramatically in her writing.
    d. getting a hug or a "high five" from each of your students as they enter the classroom in the morning.

5. Autonomy—being in control of one's existence—is best described as an
    a. intrinsic reward in teaching.
    b. emotional reward in teaching.
    c. extrinsic reward in teaching.
    d. intellectual reward in teaching.

6. Which of the following best describes teacher status?
    a. Teacher status is low, so it is a difficulty in teaching.
    b. Teacher status is high, so it is an emotional reward in teaching.
    c. Teacher status is quite high, so it is an intellectual reward in teaching.
    d. Teacher status is quite high, so it is an extrinsic reward in teaching.

7. Which of the following best describes teacher work schedules?
    a. They're extrinsic rewards in teaching.
    b. They're emotional rewards in teaching.
    c. They're difficulties in teaching.
    d. They're intellectual rewards in teaching.

8. Of the following the most important reason teachers leave the profession is
    a. unfavorable work schedules.
    b. lack of autonomy.
    c. job stress.
    d. low-achieving students.

9. Teachers are often concerned about unsupportive administrators, parents who don't support teachers' efforts, and students who are disruptive and unmotivated. Of the following these difficulties are best classified as
   a. factors that detract from teachers' status.
   b. factors that reduce teachers' autonomy.
   c. factors that reduce the intellectual rewards in teaching.
   d. factors that make teachers' working conditions difficult.

10. Which of the following do teachers most commonly cite as a difficulty?
    a. Working with colleagues and administrators who lack human relations skills
    b. Spending so much time on nonteaching duties like filling out student progress reports that they don't have time to teach
    c. Spending so much time with parents of low-achieving students that they don't have time to effectively organize instruction
    d. Spending so much time in faculty meetings that they don't have enough preparation time

11. Of the following which statement most accurately describes the issue of teacher salaries?
    a. Teacher salaries are frequently cited as a major reason people leave teaching, but salaries are improving.
    b. Teacher salaries, the most common reason people leave teaching, are falling further and further behind those of other professions.
    c. Teacher salaries are rapidly improving and are now on a par with those of other professions like engineering.
    d. Teacher salaries start lower than those of other professions but catch up after 5 years of experience.

12. Which of the following is closest to the average yearly teacher salary in the United States?
    a. $25,000
    b. $35,000
    c. $45,000
    d. $55,000

13. Which of the following is closest to the average beginning teacher salary in the United States?
    a. $20,000
    b. $25,000
    c. $30,000
    d. $35,000

14. Which of the following are forms of merit pay:
    (1) Money that is awarded to schools because students' test scores in the schools increased
    (2) Money that is awarded to teachers for needed materials such as supplementary textbooks
    (3) Money that is added to teachers' base salaries for teaching in high-need areas, such as math, science, and special education
    (4) Money that is added to teachers' base salaries based on principals' evaluations

    a. 1, 2, 3, 4
    b. 1, 3, 4
    c. 1, 2, 4
    d. 3, 4

15. Of the following which best describes teachers' feelings about merit pay?
    a. Teachers overwhelmingly favor merit pay; about 95 percent are in favor.
    b. Teachers generally favor merit pay; about two thirds are in favor.
    c. Teachers have mixed reactions about merit pay; about half are in favor.
    d. Teachers are generally opposed to merit pay; about two thirds are opposed.

16. Of the following what is the best description of teacher salaries in private schools compared to those in public schools?
   a. Teacher salaries in private schools are slightly higher (about 2%–5%) than teacher salaries in public schools.
   b. Teacher salaries in private schools are lower (about 30%) than salaries in public schools.
   c. Teacher salaries in private schools are approximately the same as teacher salaries in public schools.
   d. Teacher salaries in private schools are slightly lower (about 2%–5%) than teacher salaries in public schools.

17. Which of the following are commonly cited as reasons for teachers preferring to teach in a private school rather than a public school:
   (1) Higher salaries
   (2) Smaller classes
   (3) Smaller school bureaucracy
   (4) Greater parental involvement

   a. 1, 2, 4
   b. 1, 2, 3, 4
   c. 2, 3, 4
   d. 1, 3, 4

18. If you teach in a typical school, the number of students per class you can most likely expect is
   a. 15–20.
   b. 20–25.
   c. 25–35.
   d. 35–40.

19. The student–teacher ratio (number of students per teacher) is best described as a(n)
   a. physical condition of teaching.
   b. psychological condition of teaching.
   c. intrinsic condition of teaching.
   d. extrinsic condition of teaching.

20. Which of the following is the best label for this description: "A developing aspect of teaching characterized by a specialized body of knowledge, emphasis on decision making, reflection, autonomy, and ethical standards for conduct"?
   a. Pedagogical content knowledge
   b. General pedagogical knowledge
   c. Reflection
   d. Professionalism

21. Which of the following are considered to be characteristics of a profession:
   (1) A specialized body of knowledge
   (2) Extended training for licensure
   (3) Autonomy on the job
   (4) Supervision by superiors
   (5) Ethical standards for conduct

   a. 1, 2, 3, 4
   b. 1, 2, 3, 5
   c. 2, 3, 4, 5
   d. 1, 2, 4, 5

22. Teaching skills, such as questioning or the ability to organize and maintain orderly classrooms, is best described as
  a. knowledge of content.
  b. pedagogical content knowledge.
  c. general pedagogical knowledge.
  d. knowledge of learners and learning.

23. Understanding the social, historical, philosophical, organizational, and legal aspects of teaching, together with the ability and inclination to continue to learn, is best described as
  a. pedagogical content knowledge.
  b. general pedagogical knowledge.
  c. knowledge about teachers and learners.
  d. knowledge of the profession.

24. Goal-oriented problem solving based on professional knowledge is best described as demonstrating
  a. decision making.
  b. ethical behavior.
  c. pedagogical content knowledge.
  d. knowledge of the profession.

25. "A person who uses specific skills to complete well-defined tasks" best describes a
  a. professional.
  b. school principal.
  c. school guidance counselor.
  d. technician.

26. Before they are allowed to teach, most teacher candidates must complete a prescribed set of experiences that usually include earning a bachelor's degree (sometimes in a content area, such as history), completing a clinical experience such as an internship, and passing an examination. If candidates successfully complete these requirements, they are eligible for
  a. a teaching license.
  b. an autonomous working environment.
  c. National Board certification.
  d. professional pedagogical certification.

27. Which of the following terms best fits the idea of "descriptions of moral standards for good behavior"?
  a. Professionalism
  b. Rewards
  c. Autonomy
  d. Ethics

28. Consider the following statement: "The educator strives to help each student realize his or her potential as a worthy and effective member of society." Of the following which is the best description of the statement?
  a. It is a statement describing the characteristics of teachers as professionals.
  b. It is a statement describing the intrinsic rewards in teaching.
  c. It is a statement describing a principle from a Code of Ethics.
  d. It is a statement describing the autonomy of teachers as they practice their craft.

29. Some leaders argue that teaching is not a profession. Which of the following are statements these leaders make in defending this position:
 (1) Teachers lack rigorous training.
 (2) Teaching isn't an important institution in our society.
 (3) Teachers lack a unique function.
 (4) Teachers don't have the autonomy characteristic of professionals.
 (5) Teachers aren't held accountable for student learning.

    a.   1, 2, 3, 4
    b.   1, 2, 3, 5
    c.   2, 3, 4, 5
    d.   1, 3, 4, 5

30. Critics of education argue that teaching isn't a profession because teachers aren't held accountable for student learning. Which of the following is the most accurate statement related to this assertion?
    a.   Just as teachers don't lose their jobs if their students don't meet prescribed standards, physicians also don't lose their rights to practice if a prescribed medication fails to improve a patient's condition.
    b.   Although the statement is true at the present time, teaching will become a profession if and when teachers are held accountable for their students' learning.
    c.   The statement is false, since high-stakes tests are now being given in most states so that teachers are now being held accountable for student learning.
    d.   The statement is irrelevant because student learning is impossible to measure, making teacher accountability also impossible.

31. "Suggested changes in teaching and teacher preparation intended to increase the amount students learn" are best described as
    a.   codes of ethics.
    b.   increasing professionalism.
    c.   standards-based education.
    d.   reforms.

32. We best describe teachers who are "thoughtful, analytical, and even self-critical about their teaching" as
    a.   artistic.
    b.   reflective.
    c.   scientific.
    d.   practical.

33. "Focusing curriculum and instruction on predetermined criteria" best describes
    a.   accountability.
    b.   standards-based education.
    c.   educational reforms.
    d.   codes of ethics.

34. Requiring students to demonstrate that they have met specified standards or that they demonstrate understanding of the topics they study as measured by standardized tests and holding teachers responsible for students' learning best describes
    a.   teacher autonomy.
    b.   accountability.
    c.   educational reform.
    d.   high-stakes tests.

35. The PRAXIS series is best described as
   a. support given first-year teachers to help them make the transition into the classroom.
   b. experiences provided for teachers that allow them to practice classroom skills.
   c. a test given to teachers designed to measure their readiness for teaching.
   d. a series of moral dilemmas designed to measure teachers' understanding of their professional codes of ethics.

36. Of the following the most accurate meaning of the term *PRAXIS* is
   a. putting theory into practice.
   b. practicing skills in schools.
   c. providing support for first-year teachers.
   d. exit criteria for teachers.

37. Which of the following is the best description of the statement "The teacher understands how children learn and develop and can provide learning opportunities that support their intellectual, social, and personal development?"
   a. It is a statement taken from the NEA Code of Ethics.
   b. It is a description of one of the INTASC principles.
   c. It is a statement taken from the description of the No Child Left Behind Act.
   d. It is a statement taken from the description of teachers as advanced professionals.

38. Which of the following is the best description of the No Child Left Behind Act?
   a. It is an amendment to the National Education Association Code of Ethics.
   b. It is one of the INTASC principles.
   c. It is an attempt by several states to increase the professionalism of teaching.
   d. It is an accountability reform sponsored by the federal government.

39. Which of the following are accountability provisions of the No Child Left Behind Act:
   (1) All states are required to create standards for what every child should know at all grades.
   (2) Independent agencies (agencies outside school districts) sponsored by the federal government will determine the extent to which standards are being met.
   (3) Students attending schools that fail to make adequate yearly progress for 2 years in a row can transfer to another school.
   (4) Schools, districts, and states must keep records of performance to document achievement of different groups of students by race, ethnicity, gender, and English proficiency.

   a. 1, 2, 3, 4
   b. 1, 3, 4
   c. 1, 2, 4
   d. 1, 4

40. Of the following the most common criticism directed at high-stakes tests is
   a. the tests fail to measure achievement in important areas of the curriculum, and as a result they aren't a valid measure of student achievement.
   b. the tests are very time consuming and difficult for teachers to grade.
   c. the tests narrow the curriculum by forcing teachers to focus primarily on the subjects measured by the tests.
   d. the tests take too much time to administer and score, leaving teachers with less time to devote to instruction.

Items for Analysis and Critical Thinking

41. Jana Juarez illustrates the concept of dominant and recessive genes by playing two radios simultaneously. The students can hear one but not the other. As Jana questions the students, she reminds them that both radios are playing but the sound of one drowns out the other. Jana's ability to represent a topic like genetics in this way best illustrates
   a. knowledge of content.
   b. pedagogical content knowledge.
   c. general pedagogical knowledge.
   d. knowledge of learners and learning.

42. "I don't understand why they can't seem to be able to use longitude and latitude to find exact locations," Kominko Jones, a seventh-grade geography teacher, said to herself out loud, seeing that her students weren't doing well on a quiz. "I don't think I went through enough examples," she thought. "They're trying to simply memorize some rules. I'm going to reteach it next week, and I'm going to do it differently. I know that I can get them to understand it." Of the following which is the best description of Kominko's thinking?
   a. She is demonstrating pedagogical content knowledge.
   b. She is demonstrating general pedagogical knowledge.
   c. She is demonstrating a high level of ethics.
   d. She is demonstrating a reflective attitude.

Use the following vignette for Items 43 and 44:

Four teachers were talking in the teachers' lounge. "What are you doing?" Manuel asked.

   "I just got my *Elementary School Journal* today," Juanita responded. "They always have an article or two that help me. This one has a good article on what we can do to get kids from disadvantaged backgrounds to be more conscientious about their work. I work so hard, but I really need the help."

   "Wow, impressive," Manuel waved. "How in the world do you have time to read journals? I can barely keep my head above water with all the paperwork."

   "Me, too," said David, who was sitting nearby. "Besides, there isn't much we can do for some of these kids. Doing extra reading isn't going to help all that much. I'd rather have someone tell me how to get them to behave."

   "It isn't quite that bad," Rey retorted. "I know these kids have trouble, but we have to try as hard as possible to help them."

43. Based on the evidence in the vignette, the teacher who displayed behavior *most* characteristic of a professional was
   a. Manuel.
   b. Juanita.
   c. David.
   d. Rey.

44. Based on the evidence in the vignette, the teacher who displayed behavior *least* characteristic of a professional was
   a. Manuel.
   b. Juanita.
   c. David.
   d. Rey.

45. Kevin is a very difficult student. In spite of using every technique you know, you have difficulty in preventing him from disrupting your class. In response to your frustration with him, Jack, one of your colleagues, says, "I hate doing it, but sometimes we have no choice. You simply have to put him down. I had him last year, and embarrassing him was the only thing that worked. You may have to go that far." Of the following what is the best assessment of Jack's suggestion?

    a. His suggestion is consistent with teachers' professional code of ethics, since one student doesn't have the right to disrupt the learning for others.

    b. His suggestion is not consistent with teachers' professional code of ethics, since the code says that a teacher "shall not intentionally expose the student to embarrassment."

    c. His suggestion is consistent with teachers' professional code of ethics, since the code says that "the education profession is vested by the public with a trust and responsibility requiring the highest ideals of professional service."

    d. His suggestion is not consistent with teachers' professional code of ethics, since teachers are responsible for maintaining a safe and orderly classroom.

46. "I'm going to use a paragraph," Manuel Maniere thought as he started writing a vignette to illustrate the concept of adjectives. "They think that adjectives are words that go just before nouns, and plus, they understand parts of speech better if they're in context. I'll use *exciting* because it comes after a noun, and I'll use *running* because it looks like a verb, and *home* looks like a noun. Then I'll use words like *soon, very,* and *incredibly,* as nonexamples since they're adverbs. The following is the paragraph he wrote to use in his lesson:

John and Karen drove together in his old car to the football game. They soon met their very best friends, Latoya and Michael, at the large gate near the entrance. The game was incredibly exciting, and because the team's running game was in high gear, the home team won by a bare margin.

Of the following Manuel's efforts best illustrate

    a. general pedagogical knowledge.

    b. professional ethics.

    c. knowledge of the profession.

    d. decision making.

Use the following vignette for Items 47 and 48:

Students at Baker County High School (BCHS) all have to pass the Comprehensive Assessment Measure (CAM), which focuses on reading, writing, and math. BCHS is "graded" on the students' performance, and the school receives bonus funds from the state if BCHS students perform well on the CAM. Students are not allowed to graduate from high school until they reach a prescribed level of performance on the measure.

47. Of the following the CAM is best described as a(n)

    a. educational reform.

    b. type of accountability.

    c. high-stakes test.

    d. prescribed standard.

48. Teachers at BCHS are responsible for students' performance on the CAM. Holding teachers responsible in this way best illustrates

    a. standards-based education.

    b. accountability.

    c. educational reform.

    d. teacher autonomy.

49. Juan, a preservice teacher, is in the process of collecting evidence of his work in schools. He has a box into which he has put a lesson plan that he used when he taught a lesson in math, the examples he used to illustrate the topic he taught, a videotape of the lesson, and written feedback about the lesson from his directing teacher. He is now in the process of doing the same thing in language arts and science. Of the following which is the best description of Juan's efforts?
    a.   He is preparing pedagogical content knowledge.
    b.   He is demonstrating accountability.
    c.   He is responding to a high-stakes test.
    d.   He is preparing a professional portfolio.

Extended-Response Items

50. Identify the two most commonly cited reasons people give for choosing teaching as a career. What is the most likely explanation for these reasons? (4 points)

51. Describe three different kinds of rewards in teaching. Give a specific, concrete example of each. (6 points)

52. Describe two different difficulties in teaching. Give a specific example of each. (4 points)

53. Describe the characteristics of a profession. Provide an example that illustrates each of the characteristics. (8 points)

54. Describe each of the types of knowledge that teachers must possess to be effective. Give a specific example of each. (8 points)

55. Take one of the following positions: (1) teaching is a profession, or (2) teaching is not a profession. Cite specific evidence in support of the position you take. (8 points)

56. Critics of high-stakes testing raise three issues with respect to the testing of cultural minorities. Identify and explain the issues. (6 points)

CHAPTER TWO

THE TEACHING PROFESSION

Knowledge-Level Items

1. Which of the following best describes a trend in the prevalence of summer school for K–12 students in the United States?
    a. Summer school is rapidly expanding across the country because of increasing accountability.
    b. Summer school is expanding in the inner cities but is decreasing in other parts of the country.
    c. Summer school remains at about the same level as it has been for the last 20 years.
    d. Summer school is decreasing because parents object to summer vacations being disrupted.

2. Some educational leaders advocate increasing the amount of time students spend in school, arguing that the more time students spend in learning activities the more they will learn. Of the following which is the most valid assessment of this argument based on research?
    a. The argument is valid; in general the more time students spend in school the more they learn.
    b. The argument is valid for low-achieving students but not for high-achieving students; the more time low achievers spend in school the more they learn, but no positive effect of lengthening the school year has been found for high achievers.
    c. The argument is valid for high-achieving students but not for low-achieving students; the more time high achievers spend in school the more they learn, but no positive effect of lengthening the school year has been found for low achievers.
    d. The argument is not valid; in general, lengthening the school year has not resulted in any significant learning increases for students.

3. Of the following which is the best description of *modified school calendars*?
    a. Calendars that increase the length of the school year by adding days beyond the traditional 180 days
    b. Calendars that increase the length of the school year by making summer school mandatory
    c. Calendars that increase the number of days students spend in school by shortening traditional vacations, such as the long winter holiday and spring break
    d. Calendars that eliminate long summer holidays without changing the total length of the school year

4. Of the following which statement is the most commonly cited argument supporting modified school calendars?
    a. Modified calendars help prevent the negative impact of long summer vacations on learning ("summer loss").
    b. Teachers prefer modified calendars to the traditional calendar.
    c. Students and their parents prefer modified calendars to the traditional calendar.
    d. The cost of operating schools on modified calendars is less than the cost of traditional calendars.

5. Of the following which is the most commonly cited objection to modified school calendars?
    a. Teachers lack the energy to work with students throughout the calendar year.
    b. Parents resist intrusions on family vacations and other family activities.
    c. Schools lack the administrative staff to run schools throughout the calendar year.
    d. Students need a long summer break to assimilate what they've learned during the traditional 180-day school year.

6. In the United States the 40-hour work week is the norm. Which of the following statements, as a comparison to this norm, best describes typical teacher work weeks?
    a. Teachers' work weeks are slightly shorter than the 40-hour norm.
    b. Teachers' work weeks are approximately equal to the 40-hour norm (about 38–44 hours per week).
    c. Teachers' work weeks are slightly longer than the 40-hour norm (about 45–50 hours per week).
    d. Teachers' work weeks are much longer than the 40-hour norm (50–60 hours per week).

7. Which of the following statements best describes the length of American teachers' work weeks compared to that of other occupations in the United States requiring bachelor degrees?
   a. Teachers' work weeks are slightly shorter than the work weeks of other occupations requiring bachelor degrees (about 38–44 hours per week).
   b. Teachers' work weeks are approximately equal to the work weeks of other occupations requiring bachelor degrees (about 45 hours per week).
   c. Teachers' work weeks are slightly longer than the work weeks of other occupations requiring bachelor degrees (about 50 hours per week).
   d. Teachers work weeks are much longer than the work weeks of other occupations requiring bachelor degrees (55–60 hours per week).

8. Which of the following best describes the approximate percentage of a teacher's workday that is spent with students?
   a. About 25 percent
   b. About 50 percent
   c. About 75 percent
   d. About 90 percent

9. Which of the following statements best describes the amount of time Japanese teachers spend directly involved in classroom instruction with students, compared to that of teachers in the United States?
   a. Japanese teachers spend only about half the time that American teachers spend directly involved in instruction (with the rest spent on planning and conferring with colleagues).
   b. Japanese teachers spend slightly less time (about 10% less) than American teachers spend directly involved in instruction.
   c. Japanese teachers spend about the same amount of time as American teachers spend directly involved in instruction.
   d. Japanese teachers spend significantly more time (about 25% more) than American teachers spend directly involved in instruction.

10. Which of the following statements best describes the professionalism of Japanese teachers compared to the professionalism of American teachers?
   a. Japanese teachers are significantly less professional than American teachers, since they spend so much time in direct instruction that their autonomy is limited.
   b. The professionalism of Japanese teachers is similar to the professionalism of American teachers, since they are directly involved in instruction about the same percentage of the time and have about the same degree of autonomy.
   c. Japanese teachers are slightly more professional than American teachers, since they spend a slightly smaller percentage of their time in direct instruction and have more autonomy than do American teachers.
   d. Japanese teachers are significantly more professional than American teachers, since they spend only about half as much time in instruction and thus have much more autonomy and are more involved in school governance.

11. Which of the following best describes the length of the school year in Japan compared to the length of the school year in the United States?
   a. The length of the school year in Japan is significantly shorter than that in the United States (about 150 days in Japan compared to about 180 days in the United States).
   b. The length of the school year in Japan is about the same as that in the United States (about 180 days).
   c. The length of the school year in Japan is slightly longer than that in the United States (about 200 days in Japan compared to about 180 days in the United States).
   d. The length of the school year in Japan is significantly longer than that in the United States (about 240 days in Japan compared to about 180 days in the United States).

12. Which of the following best describes *block schedules*?
    a. Organizing different content areas, such as math and science, into interdisciplinary blocks in junior high and high schools
    b. Creating blocks for areas such as art, music, and physical education that are not part of the core curriculum (math, language arts, social studies, and science) in elementary schools
    c. Creating blocks for basic skills areas—reading, writing, and math—in elementary schools
    d. Increasing the length of class periods, such as doubling the length of a typical class period, particularly in junior high and high schools

13. Which of the following best describes a scheduling system in which students take four classes a day that are approximately 90–100 minutes long and they complete courses in one semester that take a year in a traditional system?
    a. A rotating block schedule
    b. A four-by-four block schedule
    c. An alternating-day block schedule
    d. An integrated-day block schedule

14. Which of the following best describes a scheduling system in which classes are approximately 90–100 minutes long and students take eight classes that meet every other day per semester?
    a. A rotating block schedule
    b. A four-by-four block schedule
    c. An alternating-day block schedule
    d. An integrated-day block schedule

15. Of the following which is the most commonly cited advantage of teaching in elementary schools compared to teaching in secondary schools?
    a. Elementary schools are more personalized environments than secondary schools, and relationships with students are a source of satisfaction in teaching.
    b. Since elementary classrooms are self-contained, elementary teachers have more autonomy than do secondary teachers.
    c. Elementary teachers are generally considered to be more professional than secondary teachers.
    d. The length of elementary teachers' workdays is significantly shorter than that of secondary teachers.

16. Of the following which is the most commonly cited advantage of teaching in secondary schools compared to teaching in elementary schools?
    a. Because of departmentalization secondary teachers generally have more autonomy than do elementary teachers.
    b. Because the students are more mature, teaching in secondary schools is generally more satisfying than teaching in elementary schools.
    c. Because they have only one or two different preparations, secondary teachers' workdays are significantly shorter than the workdays of elementary teachers.
    d. Departmentalization in secondary schools provides more opportunities to focus on content areas of interest and share that interest with students.

17. "Teachers' abilities to empathize with and invest in the protection and development of young people" best describes which of the following?
    a. Withitness
    b. Overlapping
    c. Caring
    d. Artistry

18. Of the following which is the best indicator of teacher caring?
    a. Avoiding communications and learning activities that might damage learners' self-esteem
    b. Demonstrating that you respect students by holding them to high standards
    c. Designing learning activities to ensure that students are successful virtually all of the time
    d. Telling the students that you value each of them as an individual

Use the following information for Items 19 and 20:

In a study conducted by Boyer (1995), students were asked to identify characteristics of a good teacher.

19. Of the following which did they rate *most* important?
    a.   Being able to provide clear explanations of topics
    b.   Being able to maintain an orderly classroom
    c.   Being knowledgeable about what they were teaching
    d.   Being kind and friendly

20. Of the following which did they rate *least* important?
    a.   Being knowledgeable about what they were teaching
    b.   Being kind and friendly
    c.   Understanding student problems
    d.   Willingness to spend time with students after school

21. The description "constantly evaluating the effectiveness of your teaching" best describes which of the following:
    a.   Withitness
    b.   Overlapping
    c.   Reflective practitioner
    d.   Caring professional

22. A teacher's awareness of what is going on in all parts of the classroom all the time and communicating this awareness to students best describes
    a.   reflection.
    b.   withitness.
    c.   decision making.
    d.   caring.

23. Which of the following is the best description of a *productive learning environment*?
    a.   An environment in which all students know that the teacher cares about them
    b.   An environment in which all students are successful
    c.   An environment that has clear rules and standards for acceptable behavior
    d.   An environment that is orderly and focuses on learning

24. According to research examining the benefits of home-school cooperation, which of the following are ways in which students benefit from parental involvement in their children's schooling?
    (1) Higher academic achievement
    (2) More positive attitudes toward school
    (3) More acceptable student behavior
    (4) Better attendance rates
    (5) Greater willingness to do homework

    a.   1, 2, 3, 4, 5
    b.   2, 3, 4, 5
    c.   1, 2, 3, 4
    d.   1, 3, 4, 5

25. Research examining home–school cooperation has identified several barriers to parental involvement in school activities. Which of the following are most commonly identified as these barriers?
    (1) Economic barriers, such as parents holding more than one job and lacking resources such as child care or transportation to and from school
    (2) Attitude barriers, such as parents feeling home–school cooperation is unnecessary since it is the parents' job to parent and it's the school's job to educate
    (3) Cultural barriers, such as parents having attended schools that were very different from the ones their children are now attending
    (4) Language barriers, such as children coming from homes where the first language is not English

    a.   1, 2, 3, 4
    b.   2, 3, 4
    c.   1, 3, 4
    d.   1, 2, 4

26. Which of the following statements best describes standards for parents' roles in their children's learning?
    a. Parents should be involved in their children's extracurricular activities but should avoid involvement in activities directly related to what students learn in their classes.
    b. Parents should regularly communicate with the school and should play an integral role in assisting their children's learning.
    c. Parents should communicate with the school and should be involved in their children's learning, but decisions that directly affect their children's learning are left in the hands of school professionals.
    d. Parents are welcome in schools to promote communication and support for their students, but learning decisions are left in the hands of school leaders, such as principals and guidance counselors.

27. Teachers make up about what percent of the total number of school staff (with the remaining being administrators and support staff, such as secretaries and custodians) in the United States?
    a. 30
    b. 50
    c. 75
    d. 90

28. Which of the following statements best describes the percentage of total school staff that are teachers in the United States compared to that in other industrialized countries, such as Japan, Germany, Italy, and Belgium?
    a. The percentage of total school staff that are teachers in the United States is much lower than it is in other industrialized countries (about 50% in the United States, compared to between 60% and 75% in other industrialized countries.
    b. The percentage of total school staff that are teachers in the United States is about the same as the percentage in other industrialized countries (about 75% in both the United States and other industrialized countries).
    c. The percentage of total school staff that are teachers in the United States is slightly higher than it is in other industrialized countries (about 75% in the United States, compared to about 70% in other industrialized countries).
    d. The percentage of total school staff that are teachers in the United States is much higher than it is in other industrialized countries (about 75% in the United States, compared to about 50% in other industrialized countries).

29. In the United States which of the following best describes the number of men in teaching compared to that of women?
    a. Men and women each make up about half the teaching force.
    b. Women make up slightly more than half the teaching force.
    c. Women make up about three fourths of the teaching force.
    d. Women make up about 90 percent of the teaching force.

30. Attempts have been made to attract men to teaching in elementary schools. Of the following which statement most accurately describes the success of these attempts?
   a. The attempts have been totally unsuccessful since the percentage of male teachers in elementary schools has dropped significantly in the last 10 years.
   b. The attempts have been largely unsuccessful since the percentage of male teachers in elementary schools hasn't changed significantly in the last 10 years.
   c. The attempts have been somewhat successful since the percentage of male teachers in elementary schools has increased about 10 percent in the last 10 years.
   d. The attempts have been highly successful since the percentage of male teachers in elementary schools has nearly doubled in the last 10 years.

31. A man is attempting to maximize the likelihood of finding a job. Based on the distribution of men and women in teaching positions, where will his opportunities be the greatest?
   a. In an elementary school
   b. In middle school science
   c. In high school English
   d. In high school social studies

32. A woman is attempting to maximize the likelihood of finding a job. Based on the distribution of men and women in teaching positions, where will her opportunities be the greatest?
   a. In an elementary school
   b. In high school math
   c. In high school English
   d. In special education

33. Consider the percentage of cultural minorities, such as African Americans or Hispanics, in the teaching population. Which of the following statements is most accurate?
   a. About 13 percent of the teaching force is made up of cultural minorities, but the percentage is increasing rapidly (about a 10% increase per year).
   b. About 13 percent of the teaching force is made up of cultural minorities, and the percentage is increasing slightly (about a 2% increase per year).
   c. About 13 percent of the teaching force is made up of cultural minorities, and the percentage has remained constant for the last 10 years.
   d. About 13 percent of the teaching force is made up of cultural minorities, but the percentage has decreased slightly over the last 10 years.

34. The small percentage of cultural minorities in the teaching force has some school leaders concerned. Which of the following is the most commonly cited reason for this concern?
   a. Research indicates that cultural minorities are generally more empathetic in dealing with students than are nonminorities.
   b. Research indicates that cultural minorities generally have a better grasp of the content they're teaching than do nonminorities.
   c. Research indicates that cultural minorities better manage classrooms (i.e., maintain acceptable student behavior) than do nonminorities.
   d. Research indicates that the minority student population is rapidly increasing, and leaders believe they need minority teachers as role models.

35. A number of school leaders encourage the active recruitment of cultural minorities for the teaching force. Which of the following are reasons given for encouraging this active recruitment?
    (1) The need for minority role models
    (2) The need for effective instructors of minority students
    (3) The need for teachers who are knowledgeable in particular content areas
    (4) The need for alternative perspectives

     a.   1, 2, 3, 4
     b.   2, 3, 4
     c.   1, 3, 4
     d.   1, 2, 4

36. Which of the following statements best describes teachers now entering the teaching force, compared to existing teachers?
     a.   Teachers now entering the workforce are more likely to be male, younger, and a member of a cultural minority than those presently teaching.
     b.   Teachers now entering the workforce are more likely to be female, older, and a member of a cultural minority than those presently teaching.
     c.   Teachers now entering the workforce are more likely to be male, younger, and white than those presently teaching.
     d.   Teachers now entering the workforce are more likely to be female, younger, and white than those presently teaching.

37. When teachers describe themselves as dissatisfied with their careers, which of the following is the most frequently cited reason?
     a.   Low salaries (salaries that are much lower than the salaries of other professionals)
     b.   Lack of rewards in teaching (such as lack of personal or intellectual rewards)
     c.   Difficult working conditions (such as problems with student discipline)
     d.   Lack of opportunity for career advancement (such as no increases in professional rank for veteran teachers)

38. By the end of their third year, which of the following best describes the percentage of teachers who leave the profession?
     a.   15 percent
     b.   25 percent
     c.   40 percent
     d.   75 percent

Items for Analysis and Critical Thinking

Consider the complexities of teaching as you read the following vignette, and then use this information to respond to Items 39–44.

Juan Alvarez is a fifth-grade teacher in an urban elementary school. He has 26 students, 4 of whom are absent, and he is working with a reading group of 8 while the remaining 14 are working on a seatwork assignment. As Karen reads aloud, Juan sees Bill tapping Louanne on the back of her head with a pencil. Karen finishes, and Juan then asks Ariel to read as he continues to watch Bill and Louanne. Bill taps Louanne again, and she flails her arm back trying to hit him, just as the intercom says, "Mr. Alvarez?"

     "Yes," Juan responds.
     "Is Clarice Torres in your class today?"
     "Yes, she is."
     "Would you please send her down to the office?"
     "Clarice," Juan says nodding to her, smiling inwardly since announcements commonly occur during his reading period.

Clarice gets up and heads out the door, Juan tells Ariel to continue, and he gets up, goes over to Bill and Louanne, and warns Bill that another incident of misbehavior will result in a call to his mother. Several of the students doing seatwork look up as Juan admonishes Bill and hears Juan say that Bill's mother is likely to be called. Juan then returns to his reading group as he watches to be sure that Bill is working on his seatwork.

39. The combination of a reading group in progress, students working on a seatwork assignment, and an intercom announcement best illustrates which of the following?
   a.   The multidimensional aspect of teaching
   b.   The public aspect of teaching
   c.   The unpredictable aspect of teaching
   d.   The artistic aspect of teaching

40. Juan's feeling that it was necessary to leave his reading group to intervene in the incident between Bill and Louanne best illustrates which of the following?
   a.   The multidimensional aspect of teaching
   b.   The immediate aspect of teaching
   c.   The public aspect of teaching
   d.   The artistic aspect of teaching

41. The progress of the reading group, the students doing seatwork, the incident between Bill and Louanne, and the intercom all occurred at virtually the same time. The fact that they did so best illustrates which of the following?
   a.   The immediate aspect of teaching
   b.   The artistic aspect of teaching
   c.   The public aspect of teaching
   d.   The simultaneous aspect of teaching

42. The fact that several of the students looked up when Juan admonished Bill best illustrates which of the following?
   a.   The immediate aspect of teaching
   b.   The multidimensional aspect of teaching
   c.   The public aspect of teaching
   d.   The simultaneous aspect of teaching

43. Even though he was conducting a reading group, Juan saw Bill tapping Louanne the first time he did it. Juan's awareness of all the simultaneous events occurring in the classroom best illustrates which of the following?
   a.   His withitness
   b.   His understanding of the public aspect of teaching
   c.   His artistry as a teacher
   d.   His pedagogical content knowledge

44. The progress of Juan's reading group was not interrupted when he intervened in the incident between Bill and Louanne. His ability to do both at the same time best illustrates which of the following concepts?
   a.   Withitness
   b.   Teacher artistry
   c.   Pedagogical content knowledge
   d.   Overlapping

45. "What are you doing?" Enrique asked Monica as Monica was laboring over a paper. "Mrs. Aguilar made me do this over," Monica responded. "She said it was full of spelling and grammar and punctuation mistakes, and she wouldn't accept it." "Was it?" Enrique continued. ". . . I guess so," Monica responded, a bit sheepishly. Of the following which is the best description of Mrs. Aguilar's actions with Monica?

    a. She is demonstrating withitness by catching Monica's sloppy work and making Monica do it again.

    b. She is demonstrating overlapping by first assigning the paper and then making Monica do it a second time.

    c. She is demonstrating that she respects Monica by not accepting sloppy work.

    d. She is demonstrating the multidimensional nature of teaching by having Monica do a single assignment twice.

Use the following information for Items 46–50:

Susan Wilson arrives at school an hour early each morning "to be sure I have my act together." She arranges her room and checks to be sure that she has her materials ready so that the minute she wants to begin a lesson, she only has to grab the stuff off her shelf. Today, she is going to do a lesson on place value in math with her second graders, and she has a number of popsicle sticks on her shelf, each of which has ten beans glued to it. She also has a number of beans in a can that she uses for "ones" in her lesson on place value.

Susan also checks to be sure that her student packets are ready, since it's Friday, and Friday is the day that she sends packets of student work home to parents, which they must sign and return on Monday. As soon as she's finished, she looks at her daily planner and nods to herself, "Oh yes, we have a curriculum meeting after school Monday." The school is considering a new math series, and the second-grade team is being asked to provide their input to the school's curriculum committee by the end of the following week.

"Too much to do," she mumbles, half aloud. "I really want to go see what this guy the district is bringing in is saying about math instruction in Japanese schools," she thinks. "They're supposed to be so great; I want to find out what they're doing."

"I need to get some more crackers," she says to herself out loud as she opens the bottom drawer of her desk. She keeps a box of crackers in her desk for her children, because one or two of them come to school every day without having eaten any breakfast. "Crackers aren't perfect," she thinks wryly, "but they're better than eating nothing at all."

46. Of the following Susan's making a point to have a box of crackers in her desk best illustrates which role of teaching?

    a. The caring professional role

    b. The creator of productive learning environments

    c. The ambassador to the public

    d. The collaborative colleague

    e. The learner and reflective practitioner

47. Of the following Susan's meeting with her grade team best illustrates which role of teaching?

    a. The caring professional

    b. The creator of productive learning environments

    c. The ambassador to the public

    d. The collaborative colleague

    e. The learner and reflective practitioner

48. Susan arrived early to school, and she checked to see if she had her materials ready for her lesson on place value. This behavior best illustrates which role of teaching?

    a. The caring professional

    b. The creator of productive learning environments

    c. The ambassador to the public

    d. The collaborative colleague

    e. The learner and reflective practitioner

49. Susan routinely sent packets of student work home to parents, requiring that the parents sign the packets to confirm that they had inspected the work and return the materials to school. Of the following this procedure best illustrates which role of teaching?
   a. The caring professional
   b. The creator of productive learning environments
   c. The ambassador to the public
   d. The collaborative colleague
   e. The learner and reflective practitioner

50. Susan's wanting to hear the speaker describe math instruction in Japanese schools best illustrates which role of teaching?
   a. The caring professional
   b. The creator of productive learning environments
   c. The ambassador to the public
   d. The collaborative colleague
   e. The learner and reflective practitioner

Extended-Response Items

51. Compare the amount of time teachers in Japan spend directly involved in classroom instruction to the amount American teachers spend directly involved in instruction. Does this suggest that Japanese teachers are treated more or less like professionals than are American teachers? Cite specific evidence in defense of your position. (6 points)

52. Describe two different types of block schedules that are commonly used in American junior high and high schools. Identify three advantages that proponents cite in suggesting that schools use block scheduling. (5 points)

53. Identify four different dimensions of classroom life that make teaching complex and demanding. Include a specific example to illustrate each. (8 points)

54. Identify four different roles required of teachers. Cite a specific example that illustrates each of the roles. (8 points)

55. Describe the existing teaching force. In your description identify the approximate percentage of women as compared to men, the percentage of cultural minorities, and the average age. (3 points)

56. Compare people who are now entering the teaching force to those already teaching. In your comparison address gender, culture (cultural minorities compared to nonminorities), and age. (3 points)

57. Many school leaders are encouraging the recruitment of cultural minorities into the teaching force. Cite three reasons that they give for encouraging these efforts. Explain each reason. (6 points)

CHAPTER THREE

LEARNER DIVERSITY: DIFFERENCES IN TODAY'S STUDENTS

Knowledge-Level Items

1. The attitudes, values, customs, and behavior that characterize a social group are best described as
    a. culture.
    b. ethnicity.
    c. exceptionalities.
    d. socioeconomic status.

2. A person's ancestry and the way individuals identify themselves with the nation from which they or their ancestors came is best described as
    a. culture.
    b. ethnicity.
    c. exceptionalities.
    d. socioeconomic status.

3. Consider the following ethnic groups: Hispanic, African American, Asian/Pacific Islander, American Indian/Alaskan Native and Non-Hispanic White. Experts estimate that by 2020 significant increases will occur in the percentage of the school population in each of these groups except one, and this one will decrease in percentage. The group that will decrease in percentage is
    a. Hispanic.
    b. African American.
    c. Asian/Pacific Islander.
    d. Non-Hispanic White.

4. According to research, which of the following statements best describes students' tendencies to drop nonstandard English dialects in favor of standard English?
    a. Students quickly drop nonstandard dialects because they don't want to appear as if they aren't "cool" or "withit" to their peers.
    b. Students quickly drop nonstandard dialects because the school curriculum uses standard English.
    c. Students are sometimes reluctant to drop nonstandard dialects in favor of standard English because the nonstandard dialect is the language of the home.
    d. Students are sometimes reluctant to drop nonstandard dialects in favor of standard English for fear of alienating peers.

5. Which of the following statements best describes "resistance cultures"?
    a. Cultural characteristics that detract from a group's assimilation into American culture
    b. Ability differences that detract from a student's success in school activities
    c. Peer values that don't support, and sometimes actually oppose, school learning
    d. Learner exceptionalities that make acquiring certain skills, such as reading, difficult

6. Researchers have attempted to understand the high success rates of Southeast Asian students who have been in the United States a relatively short period of time. Of the following which is the most accurate description of the researchers' findings?
    a. The researchers found that the families of these children placed heavy emphasis on the importance of education and hard work.
    b. The researchers found that these children were innately superior to American children as measured by intelligence tests.
    c. The researchers found that, because the children's families had come from war-torn areas, teachers gave the children added support and attention.
    d. The researchers found that the children had virtually no involvement in extracurricular activities, so they devoted all their energies to academics.

7. Researchers have examined the effects of teachers changing their instruction so they ask more open-ended questions, such as "What do you notice about the information on the overhead?" instead of asking questions requiring specific answers. Which of the following is the most accurate description of the effects of this change in instruction?
   a. The participation of African American students in the class increased.
   b. The participation of African American students in the class was not changed.
   c. The participation of African American students was not changed but the answers the students gave to the open-ended questions indicated less thought on the part of the students.
   d. The participation of African American students decreased.

8. The process of socializing cultural minorities so that their behaviors fit the social patterns of the majority is best described as
   a. cultural inversion.
   b. assimilation.
   c. multicultural education.
   d. culturally responsive teaching.

9. Evidence indicates that the concept of America as a melting pot never fully occurred. Which of the following statements provides the best evidence indicating that America never was a true and complete melting pot?
   a. Neighborhoods and groups continue to celebrate unique cultural festivals and maintain cultural habits.
   b. Many people came to the United States as non-native English speakers.
   c. The number of minority students in America's schools is rapidly increasing.
   d. The achievement of some minority groups tends to lag behind the achievement of white students.

10. "A variety of strategies schools use to accommodate cultural differences and provide educational opportunities for all students" is best described as
   a. cultural inversion.
   b. cultural assimilation.
   c. cultural accommodation.
   d. multicultural education.

11. Which of the following are considered to be characteristics of culturally responsive teaching?
   (1) Accepting and valuing differences among ethnic groups
   (2) Emphasizing that all ethnic groups are American
   (3) Accommodating different cultural learning styles
   (4) Building on students' cultural backgrounds
   (5) Individualizing instruction for different cultural minorities

   a. 1, 2, 3, 4, 5
   b. 2, 3, 4
   c. 1, 3, 4
   d. 1, 3, 4, 5

12. Which of the following is the most accurate description of English language learners (ELL)?
   a. Students who have developed English language proficiency
   b. Students whose first language is not English
   c. Students who are native English speakers
   d. Students who can read English but cannot yet speak English

13. Which of the following best describes the primary disadvantage of maintenance bilingual programs?
   a. They maintain the native language at the expense of English.
   b. They require teachers trained in the first language (such as a teacher who speaks Spanish).
   c. They place unreasonable learning demands on students.
   d. They maintain outmoded and ineffective ways of thinking about the world.

14. A program for ESL students in which they focus on learning English and only English is spoken best describes a(n)
    a.   maintenance program.
    b.   transition program.
    c.   immersion program.
    d.   English as a Second Language program.

15. Based on research examining the rate at which newcomers to the United States are learning English, which of the following statements is most accurate?
    a.   Newcomers are learning English at a much slower rate than they have in the past (about half as fast as they have in the past).
    b.   Newcomers are learning English at a slightly slower rate than they have in the past (about 5% slower than in the past).
    c.   Newcomers are learning English at a rate that is about equal to past rates.
    d.   Newcomers are learning English more rapidly than they have in the past.

16. As you move into your teaching career, you are almost certain to have non-native English speakers in your classroom. Which of the following is the most effective way to help your non-native English speakers as their language skills are developing?
    a.   Explain everything you do slowly and clearly so that your non-native English speakers have time to try to grasp the language.
    b.   Use as many concrete examples as possible to provide real and tangible reference points for new concepts and vocabulary.
    c.   Have students explain topics to other students in their own words, because students often better identify with other students' language than the language of the teacher.
    d.   Avoid having a classroom that is too highly structured, since some cultural groups are not comfortable in highly structured environments.

17. Which of the following is NOT true of research on gender differences?
    a.   Males are more likely to be found in remedial and special education classes.
    b.   Males score lower on tests such as the SAT and ACT.
    c.   Males receive lower grades in school.
    d.   Males earn proportionally fewer bachelor's and master's degrees.

18. According to research on gender differences, which of the following statements are true?
    (1) Boys score higher than girls on standardized tests, such as the SAT and ACT.
    (2) Boys get higher grades than girls, and they score higher on measures of writing ability.
    (3) Boys earn a higher percentage of both bachelor's and master's degrees.
    (4) Boys have more behavior problems in school than do girls.
    (5) Boys are more likely to drop out of school than are girls.

    a.   1, 2, 3, 4, 5
    b.   1, 3, 5
    c.   1, 4, 5
    d.   1, 3, 4, 5

19. Of the following what is the most likely cause of gender-role identity?
    a.   It is primarily determined by genetics, which determines not only physical characteristics but also factors such as temperament and verbal ability.
    b.   It is primarily environmental, resulting from different treatment by parents, peers, and teachers.
    c.   It is a combination of genetics and environment, with both contributing in varying degrees.
    d.   It is the result of gender-specific treatment during infancy, resulting in behavioral traits that endure throughout life.

20. Of the following which is the most likely cause of gender-stereotyped views of appropriate careers for boys and girls (such as engineering or computer science being inappropriate careers for girls)?
  a. Parental attitudes and particularly the attitudes of fathers
  b. Parental attitudes and particularly the attitudes of mothers
  c. Teachers' subconscious discouragement of nonstereotypical careers (such as a teacher's subtly discouraging a girl from majoring in engineering in college)
  d. The media portraying men's and women's careers in stereotypic ways (such as computer scientists in the media usually being portrayed as men)

21. Which of the following best describes girls' career choices in areas such as engineering or computer science?
  a. Girls historically chose not to major in these areas, but the percentage of girls who now major in them is rapidly increasing.
  b. Girls remain less than half as likely as boys to pursue careers in these areas.
  c. Girls now make up slightly less than half of the college majors in these areas.
  d. Girls now earn about 55 percent of the bachelor degrees in these areas.

22. Which of the following is the most commonly cited criticism of single-gender schools?
  a. Girls in single-gender schools take fewer science courses than they take in traditional school settings.
  b. Boys in single-gender schools have higher levels of character development than do boys in traditional school settings.
  c. Girls in single-gender schools are more apt to assume leadership roles that are often reserved for boys in traditional school settings.
  d. Both boys and girls in single-gender schools develop more gender-stereotyped attitudes of the opposite sex than they develop in traditional school settings.

23. Which of the following statements most accurately describes teachers' interaction patterns with boys and girls?
  a. Teachers ask boys more questions than girls.
  b. Teachers ask girls more questions than boys.
  c. Girls initiate more questions than do boys, so teachers interact with them more often.
  d. Teachers treat boys and girls nearly the same.

24. According to a survey conducted by the American Association of University Women (1993), what percentage of eighth through eleventh graders reported some type of sexual harassment in their schools?
  a. 15 percent
  b. 30 percent
  c. 50 percent
  d. 80 percent

25. According to research surveys, which statement best describes the experiences of homosexual students in schools?
  a. Homosexual students experience a much higher incidence of harassment than do students in general (over 90% of gay students hearing antigay comments).
  b. Homosexual students experience an incidence of harassment similar to that of heterosexual girls (about 80% having experienced some form of harassment).
  c. Homosexual students experience less harassment than heterosexual girls but more than heterosexual boys.
  d. Homosexual students experience a level of harassment similar to that of students in general, since many of their peers don't know that they're homosexual.

26. Which of the following items, or items similar to them, would likely appear on an intelligence test?
   (1) On what continent is Chile?
   (2) Who was Isaac Newton?
   (3) How are a *river* and a *plateau* alike?
   (4) A shirt priced at $36 is marked 1/3 off. When it doesn't sell, the sale price is reduced by half. What is the price after the second reduction?
   (5) How far is it from Los Angeles to New York?

    a.   1, 2, 3, 4, 5
    b.   3, 4, 5
    c.   3, 4
    d.   1, 3, 4

27. "The ability to learn, to deal with abstractions, and to solve problems" most closely relates to a description of
   a. intelligence.
   b. learning style.
   c. field dependence/independence.
   d. impulsiveness and reflectiveness.

28. Using Gardner's theory of intelligence, in which of the following dimensions would sales people be most likely to score highly?
   a. Intrapersonal intelligence
   b. Visual-spatial intelligence
   c. Logical-mathematical intelligence
   d. Interpersonal intelligence

29. Consider the issue of nature/nurture in intelligence. Which of the following statements is most accurate according to researchers?
   a. Intelligence is determined primarily by genetics, and it is only minimally alterable by experience.
   b. Intelligence is determined primarily by the environment, with genetics having only a minimal impact.
   c. Genetics and the environment both make major contributions to intelligence.
   d. Intelligence is determined primarily by genetics when children are young (such as preschool), but later the environment is much more important.

30. Within-class ability grouping is most commonly used in which of the following?
   a. Reading and math
   b. Math and science
   c. Reading and science
   d. Language arts and science

31. Research indicates that ability grouping often has negative effects on students placed in low-ability groups, resulting in lower than expected achievement. Of the following the best explanation for these results is
   a. organizing instruction is more difficult for low-ability students than it is for high ability students, and as a result achievement is lowered.
   b. low-ability students are usually more fearful of their teachers, and as a result achievement is lowered.
   c. teachers tend to have lowered expectations for low-ability students, and as a result, teachers tend to lack enthusiasm about their instruction and stress conformity more than learning.
   d. teachers of low-ability students tend to have less access to materials that enhance learning, and as a result achievement is lowered.

32. Consider the effects on low-ability students of being homogeneously grouped (i.e., grouped with other low-ability students) as compared to low-ability students being placed in classes with a variety of ability levels. Which of the following is the most accurate statement according to research?
   a. Homogeneously grouped low-ability students achieve more than low-ability students placed in classes with a variety of ability levels because of the extra help they receive in classes designed for low-ability students.
   b. Homogeneously grouped low-ability students achieve more than low-ability students placed in classes with a variety of ability levels because the pace of the classes designed for low-ability students is slow enough to allow them to keep up.
   c. Homogeneously grouped low-ability students achieve at about the same level as low-ability students placed in classes with a variety of ability levels.
   d. Homogeneously grouped low-ability students achieve less than low-ability students placed in classes with a variety of ability levels.

33. "Your preferred way of learning and processing information" best describes
   a. intelligence.
   b. culture.
   c. socioeconomic status.
   d. learning style.

34. A learner that is able to take a complex word problem in math, for example, and break it into several substeps that would make solving the problem easier would best be described as
   a. having an impulsive learning style.
   b. having a reflective learning style.
   c. being a field-dependent learner.
   d. being a field-independent learner.

35. Naomi is very good at seeing the "big picture," and she is frequently called on to put situations into a whole perspective. Of the following which is the best conclusion about Naomi's learning style?
   a. She has an impulsive learning style.
   b. She has a reflective learning style.
   c. She has a field-dependent learning style.
   d. She has a field-independent learning style.

36. According to researchers, of the following what is the best example of a cultural learning style?
   a. The tendency of some cultural groups to score lower on standardized measures of achievement.
   b. The tendency of some cultural groups to favor cooperation over competition among their members
   c. The tendency of some groups to form resistance cultures, in which peer pressure devalues school achievement
   d. The tendency of some people to score very high on some of Gardner's intelligences but not in others.

37. Based on research, which of the following is the most valid implication of learning style research for the way we teach?
   a. We should be aware that students are different and vary the way we teach.
   b. We should try to match our instruction to the individual learning styles of our students.
   c. We should assess our students' learning styles and group students according to the assessment results.
   d. We should try to do as much cooperative learning as possible, because cooperative learning capitalizes on learning style differences.

38. Students' awareness of the ways they learn most effectively and their ability to control these factors is best described as
   a. field independence.
   b. cultural inversion.
   c. learning style.
   d. metacognition.

39. Which of the following are classified as students with exceptionalities?
    (1) Students who are mentally retarded
    (2) Students who are learning disabled
    (3) Students who are behaviorally disordered
    (4) Students who are gifted and talented

        a. 1, 2, 3, 4
        b. 1, 2, 3
        c. 1, 2
        d. 1, 2, 4

40. If you have students with exceptionalities in your classes, into which of the following categories are they most likely to fall?
    a. Students with visual impairments
    b. Students with mental retardation
    c. Students with learning disabilities
    d. Students with behavioral disorders

41. Which of the following is the most accurate description of Public Law 94-142?
    a. Students with exceptionalities should be taught in as normal a school setting as possible while still meeting the students' special academic, social, and physical needs.
    b. Students with exceptionalities should be given as much extra academic assistance as necessary to accommodate their special learning needs and help them compete acceptably with nonexceptional students.
    c. Students with exceptionalities should be provided with the extra counseling services needed to help them maintain self-esteem and learn to cope with their physical, emotional, and academic exceptionalities.
    d. Students with exceptionalities must be taught by teachers with the special education and training needed to help these students reach their maximum potential.

42. Of the following the description that most closely relates to *mainstreaming* is
    a. parents are guaranteed involvement in all aspects of the evaluation of their children.
    b. students with exceptionalities must be placed in environments as similar to the regular classroom as possible.
    c. minorities must have a mainstream form of test, rather than an IQ test, as the basis for placement.
    d. all school-age children with exceptionalities must be provided free public education.

43. The major difference between mainstreaming and inclusion is that
    a. inclusion addresses both cognitive and social adaptations, whereas mainstreaming does not.
    b. mainstreaming is designed to help teachers accelerate learning for students with exceptionalities, whereas inclusion is not.
    c. inclusion is intended to provide support within the classroom for regular classroom teachers, whereas mainstreaming does not provide these services.
    d. mainstreaming provides a comprehensive web of services for learners with exceptionalities, whereas inclusion does not.

44. Which of the following is the most accurate description of students who have behavior disorders?
    a. Persistent age-inappropriate behaviors that result in social conflict, personal unhappiness, and school failure
    b. Persistent inattention and hyperactivity often associated with difficulty in a single skill area, such as reading
    c. Persistent classroom management problems, often leading to or resulting from school failure
    d. Persistent impairment in ability to adapt to the requirements of the everyday world, often associated with low self-esteem

Items for Analysis and Critical Thinking

45. Ann Henderson says to her second graders, "All right, everyone, let's put our math papers away now." Don, a white student, puts his math materials away, while Leroy, an African American student, does not. If the students' behavioral patterns are typical of white and African American students, which of the following is the most likely explanation according to research?
   a. Leroy is more likely to be disobedient than is Don, so he is more likely to disregard the directive.
   b. Leroy is more likely than Don to misread Mrs. Henderson's directive, not interpreting it as a command.
   c. Leroy is less likely than Don to be attentive, so he is more likely not to hear the directive.
   d. Leroy is more likely than Don to socialize with his peers, so he is more likely to be off-task.

46. Wayne Villegas is involved in a question-and-answer session with his fourth graders. During the lesson Wayne attempts to call on all his students as equally as possible, and he wants to ask questions and have the students answer at a quick pace to maintain all the students' attention. In the process he directs a question to Bill, a white student, and then another to Michael, one of his Native American students. If Bill and Michael fit patterns identified by research into lessons like Wayne's, which of the following is the most valid conclusion?
   a. Both Bill and Michael are likely to be attentive and responsive in the lesson.
   b. Michael is likely to be responsive, but Bill is likely to drift off.
   c. Michael is more likely than Bill to be uncomfortable in a lesson like Wayne's.
   d. Bill is more likely than Michael to be uncomfortable in a lesson like Wayne's.

Use the following information for Items 47 and 48:

Tony, a high school junior, has a somewhat difficult time in school as compared to that of his peers, particularly with word problems in math and other areas that aren't tangible. In spite of high motivation, he still struggles, and new situations and problems throw him more than they do his classmates. In order to succeed, he needs a lot of practice, and his approach is somewhat more mechanical than that of his peers. He comments, "I need to be able to 'see it' to understand it. Some of these ideas are just too abstract for me. Who cares about what would have happened if the Crusades had been more successful for Christianity? I can get it, though, if I get enough practice." When Tony gets frustrated, he retreats to his room, where he plays his guitar; he has even done some of his own arrangements. Tony is very skilled at working with people, and some of his peers turn to him as an arbitrator when clashes occur in club and other organizational meetings.

47. If we were asked to assess Tony's intelligence according to researchers' and experts' traditional conceptions of intelligence, which of the following is the most valid prediction?
   a. Tony will probably score lower on a test of intelligence than his typical peers.
   b. Tony will probably get a score on an intelligence test that is similar to that of his typical peers.
   c. Tony will probably score higher on an intelligence test than his typical peers.
   d. We don't have enough evidence in the case study to assess Tony's intelligence based on researchers' traditional conceptions of intelligence.

48. Consider Tony's intelligence according to Gardner's Theory of Intelligence. Based on information in the case study and Gardner's work, which of the following statements is most valid?
   a. Tony would be described as low in intelligence according to each of Gardner's dimensions of intelligence.
   b. Tony would be described as high in intelligence according to each of Gardner's dimensions of intelligence.
   c. Tony would be described as high in intelligence for some of Gardner's dimensions and unintelligent for the rest of the dimensions.
   d. Tony would be described as low in intelligence for some dimensions, high in intelligence for others, and information is lacking for the rest of the dimensions.

Use the following information for Items 49 and 50:

Jerome works very quickly, although he sometimes makes some errors. He is successful in many aspects of school since much of what goes on in his classes involves recall of information. Eldon, on the other hand, does well in problem-solving activities because he gives his responses in class and his answers on assignments a lot of thought before he says or writes anything.

49. Based on this information, the best conclusion of the following is
    a. Jerome has an impulsive learning style.
    b. Jerome has a reflective learning style.
    c. Jerome is a field-dependent student.
    d. Jerome is a field-independent student.

50. Based on this information, the best conclusion of the following is
    a. Eldon has an impulsive learning style.
    b. Eldon has a reflective learning style.
    c. Eldon is a field-dependent student.
    d. Eldon is a field-independent student.

51. After reading the chapter in the text, Marisa then writes an answer to each of the questions that are in the margins of the book. After writing her answers, she looks at the feedback in the student supplement. "I get it better if I actually write an answer first," she comments to her friend Helen, who reads the questions in the margins and then looks at the feedback in the student supplement. Marisa consistently scores higher on the tests and quizzes. Based on the evidence presented in the example, which of the following is the best explanation for Marisa's consistently scoring higher than Helen on tests and quizzes?
    a. Marisa is a more field-independent learner than is Helen.
    b. Marisa has higher ability than does Helen.
    c. Marisa is a more impulsive learner than is Helen.
    d. Marisa is more metacognitive than is Helen.

Extended-Response Items

52. Describe the changes expected in the makeup of the student population during the next 20 years. What implications do these changes have for you as a teacher? (4 points)

53. Describe three characteristics of culturally responsive teaching. Include a specific, concrete example to illustrate each characteristic. (6 points)

54. Describe five differences between boys and girls with respect to their classroom behavior and academic achievement. For example, boys outnumber girls in remedial English and math classes. Now, list five more differences. (5 points)

55. Describe the primary difference between Gardner's view of intelligence and traditional views of intelligence. (2 points)

56. Describe *cultural learning style,* and give an example that illustrates differences in cultural learning styles. (4 points)

CHAPTER FOUR

CHANGES IN AMERICAN SOCIETY: THEIR INFLUENCES ON TODAY'S SCHOOLS

Knowledge-Level Items

1. In America, at this point in history, the institution primarily responsible for meeting the needs of young people and helping them adapt to the world is the
   a. family.
   b. schools.
   c. church.
   d. government.

2. The "traditional" American family—a father who is the primary breadwinner, a mother who stays at home, and two school-aged children—now makes up what percentage of the households in the United States?
   a. Less than 10 percent
   b. About 25 percent
   c. About 50 percent
   d. Slightly more than 65 percent

3. Families headed by married couples now make up about what percent of all households in the United States?
   a. Less than 10 percent
   b. About 25 percent
   c. Slightly more than 50 percent
   d. Slightly more than 65 percent

4. Which of the following statements best describes the implications of the changing American family for teachers?
   a. Because in many American families both parents work, more children are affluent, so they come to school better prepared to learn.
   b. Parents spend considerably less time with their children than parents have spent in the past, so teachers receive less parental support than they have received historically.
   c. Parents are better informed about school activities than they have been in the past, so they tend to be more involved in school activities than they have been historically.
   d. Education has become politically important, so parents tend to be more politically active in school policy than they have been historically.

5. Of the following which percentage best describes the number of students you will have who come from single-parent families?
   a. 10 percent
   b. 25 percent
   c. 50 percent
   d. 75 percent

6. Which of the following are appropriate adaptations that teachers can make in response to the changing American family?
   (1) When asking students to introduce parents, use statements such as, "Please introduce the adult with you" since many students will be living with a single parent or other caregiver.
   (2) Have lower expectations for students of single parents since they are likely to have less support for schooling at home.
   (3) Be flexible with meeting times to accommodate the complex job situations of many working parents.
   (4) Refrain from calling on children from troubled homes to avoid putting them on the spot and embarrassing them.

   a. 1, 2, 3, 4
   b. 1, 2, 3
   c. 1, 2, 4
   d. 1, 3

7. When researchers and leaders express concern for children's safety, lack of supervision, excessive amounts of time watching television, and lack of support for school work, they are most likely describing which of the following?
   a. Cultural minorities
   b. Resilient children
   c. Low-SES children
   d. Latchkey children

8. Which of the following are part of the definition of socioeconomic status (SES)?
   (1) Parents' level of education
   (2) Parents' intelligence (IQ)
   (3) Parents' occupation
   (4) The amount of money parents make

   a. 1,2
   b. 1,2,3
   c. 1,2,4
   d. 1,3,4

9. Which of the following statements best describes the lower-socioeconomic class in the United States?
   a. The lower-SES class makes up about 40 percent of the U.S. population, but the percentage is decreasing rapidly.
   b. The lower-SES class makes up about 40 percent of the U.S. population, and the percentage is increasing.
   c. The lower-SES class makes up about 40 percent of the U.S. population, but since the percentage is so high, this class controls a large portion of the wealth in the country.
   d. The lower-SES class makes up about 25 percent of the U.S. population, but because of government programs the percentage is increasing.

10. Which of the following best describes people with low incomes who continually struggle with economic problems?
   a. Underclass
   b. Lower-middle class
   c. Resilient class
   d. Poverty class

11. Of the following which best describes the income defined by the federal government as the poverty line?
   a. Below approximately $8,000 in family income per year
   b. Below approximately $18,000 in family income per year
   c. Below approximately $25,000 in family income per year
   d. Below approximately $35,000 in family income per year

12. According to research which of the following patterns are true of poverty?
   (1) Most people in poverty live in inner cities.
   (2) Poverty is most common in families headed by single mothers.
   (3) Poverty is more common among cultural minorities than among nonminorities.
   (4) The largest percentage of people in poverty are children.

   a. 1, 2, 3, 4
   b. 1, 2, 3
   c. 2, 3, 4
   d. 1, 3

13. Of the following which most accurately reflects experts' estimates of the number of homeless children in the United States?
   a. Up to a quarter of a million students
   b. Up to a half million students
   c. Up to a million students
   d. Up to five million students

14. Of the following which best describes the general relationship between SES and success in college?
   a. Because of their desire to move to higher-SES levels than their parents, slightly more low-SES high school graduates earn bachelor's degrees than do high-SES high school graduates.
   b. While high-SES students perform better than low-SES students in high school, little relationship exists between SES and the completion of bachelor's degrees.
   c. About one fourth of high school graduates from lower-SES levels earn bachelor's degrees, whereas more than three fourths of students from higher-SES levels earn bachelor's degrees.
   d. Less than 10 percent of high school graduates from lower-SES levels earn bachelor's degrees, whereas nearly 90 percent of students from higher-SES levels earn bachelor's degrees.

15. Socioeconomic status influences learning through which of the following ways?
   (1) Parental attitudes and values
   (2) Cultural and ethnic practices
   (3) Interaction patterns in the home
   (4) Physical and safety needs

   a. 1, 2, 3
   b. 1, 2, 4
   c. 2, 3, 4
   d. 1, 3, 4

16. Which tends to be true of students from lower-socioeconomic-status homes?
   a. They have fewer school-related background experiences than students from higher-SES backgrounds.
   b. They are unable to learn in regular classrooms and usually are placed in classes for students with exceptionalities.
   c. They tend to gravitate to activities out of the academic mainstream, such as sports, music, and art.
   d. They tend to have more fully developed social lives than students from higher-SES backgrounds.

17. Of the following, low-SES parents tend to place the greatest emphasis on
   a. autonomy and initiative.
   b. affiliation and sensitivity.
   c. achievement and independence.
   d. conformity and obedience.

18. According to research which of the following generalizations is the most accurate comparison of high- and low-SES parents?
   a. In interacting with their children, low-SES parents are *more* likely to give reasons for their directions than are high-SES parents.
   b. In interacting with their children, low-SES parents are *less* likely to give reasons for their directions than are high-SES parents.
   c. In interacting with their children, low- and high-SES parents are *equally* likely to give reasons for their directions.

19. Of the following what is the most accurate approximation of the percentage of students who are sexually active by the time they finish high school?
   a. 10 percent
   b. 25 percent
   c. 50 percent
   d. 65 percent

20. Of the following which statement most accurately compares the teenage birthrate in the United States to that in other industrialized countries?
   a. The teenage birthrate in the United States is much lower than the teenage birthrate in other industrialized countries (about half).
   b. The teenage birthrate in the United States is slightly lower (about 10% lower) than the teenage birthrate in other industrialized countries.
   c. The teenage birthrate in the United States is about the same as the teenage birthrate in other industrialized countries.
   d. The teenage birthrate in the United States is higher than in any other industrialized country.

21. Of the following which percentage most accurately describes the number of sexually active teens who will contract a sexually transmitted disease?
   a. 10 percent
   b. 25 percent
   c. 50 percent
   d. 65 percent

22. Of the following which statement most accurately compares drug use in the homosexual student population to drug use by students in general?
   a. Drug use in the homosexual student population is much lower (about 50% less) than drug use by students in general.
   b. Drug use in the homosexual student population is about the same as drug use by students in general.
   c. Drug use in the homosexual student population is slightly higher (about 5% higher) than drug use by students in general.
   d. Drug use in the homosexual student population is much higher than drug use by students in general.

23. Homosexual students make up between 5 percent and 10 percent of the student population, but they commit 30 percent of the youth suicides each year. Of the following which is the most likely reason for this disproportionate rate?
   a. Homosexual youth are disproportionately subjects of harassment in schools, which leads to depression and suicide.
   b. Homosexual youth have an innate tendency toward depression, which often leads to suicide.
   c. Homosexual youth have a high incidence of drug use, which leads to depression and suicide.
   d. Homosexual youth tend to come from low-SES backgrounds, which leads to depression and suicide.

24. According to a survey on alcohol and other drug use, of the following what is the most accurate approximation of the number of high school seniors who reported using alcohol at some time in their high school careers?
   a. 10 percent
   b. 25 percent
   c. 60 percent
   d. 85 percent

25. Of the following which statement most accurately describes the characteristics of students most likely to use alcohol and other drugs?
   a. High achievers are more likely than low achievers to use alcohol and other drugs, because they are more involved in extracurricular activities, which is where most drug use occurs.
   b. Low achievers are more likely than high achievers to use alcohol and other drugs, because drug use is associated with other risk factors, such as low SES and family instability.
   c. High achievers are more likely than low achievers to use alcohol and other drugs, because school is often boring for them and they're looking for an outlet for their energies.
   d. Average students are more likely than either high or low achievers to use alcohol and other drugs, because high achievers are involved in programs for the gifted, low achievers have remedial programs designed for them, and average students get lost in the shuffle.

26. According to a survey on school violence, of the following what is the most accurate approximation of the number of students who report some kind of violence-related problem in their schools?
   a. 10 percent
   b. 25 percent
   c. 50 percent
   d. 75 percent

27. Of the following factors which is rated highest by parents and other taxpayers in a list of concerns about school quality?
   a. School safety
   b. Qualifications of teachers
   c. Student access to technology
   d. High student standardized-test scores

28. Of the following which students are most concerned about safety and violence in their schools?
   a. Fifth graders
   b. Eighth graders
   c. Tenth graders
   d. Twelfth graders

29. Automatic suspensions that result from school disruptions, evidence of alcohol or other drug use, or bringing weapons to school are most commonly labeled
   a. school safety programs.
   b. school-wide security programs.
   c. zero tolerance programs.
   d. drug-education programs.

30. Of the following what is the most accurate description of the result of a school program requiring students to wear uniforms?
   a. After the uniform policy was implemented, school crime dropped dramatically (about a 75% drop), and school attendance rates rose.
   b. After the uniform policy was implemented, school crime dropped (about a 25% drop), but school attendance also dropped slightly.
   c. After the uniform policy was implemented, crime rates remained about the same, and school attendance rates rose.
   d. No evidence supported the uniform policy since school crime and attendance rates remained the same as before the policy was implemented.

31. According to researchers which of the following are considered to be forms of bullying?
   (1) Face-to-face attack
   (2) Threats
   (3) Teasing about sexual orientation
   (4) Telling students that they can't play with others
   (5) Spreading malicious rumors

   a. 1, 2, 3, 4, 5
   b. 1, 2, 3, 5
   c. 1, 2, 3, 4
   d. 1, 2, 3

32. In a survey of middle school students, what percent reported being bullied several times in the last 30 days?
   a. 10 percent
   b. 25 percent
   c. 50 percent
   d. 75 percent

33. According to research which of the following is the most accurate description of bullying among girls compared to bullying among boys?
- a. Boys bully about three times more than girls.
- b. Boys bully about twice as much as girls.
- c. Boys and girls bully in about equal amounts.
- d. Girls bully about twice as much as boys.

34. Which of the following is the most accurate description of adults' responses to bullying?
- a. Adults quickly intervene to protect the victim and punish the perpetrator in cases of bullying.
- b. Adults quickly intervene to protect the victim in cases of bullying, but perpetrators are rarely punished.
- c. Adults often punish victims of bullying because they believe the victims are merely tattling.
- d. Adults rarely intervene one way or the other in incidents of bullying.

35. Of the following what is the most commonly voiced criticism of zero tolerance policies?
- a. Zero tolerance policies are ineffective because it is impossible to implement them consistently and uniformly.
- b. Zero tolerance policies are ineffective because they don't discriminate between major and minor offenses (such as a first grader being suspended for kissing a classmate).
- c. Zero tolerance policies are ineffective because it is virtually impossible to catch and convict the perpetrators of the most serious violations.
- d. Zero tolerance policies are ineffective because they are very unpopular with parents and other taxpayers.

36. Which of the following most accurately describes trends in school violence since the mid-1990s?
- a. School violence has dramatically increased, and it is now one of the most important problems facing schools.
- b. School violence has increased slightly, but steps are being taken to reduce it.
- c. The amount of school violence has remained approximately the same over this time period.
- d. School violence has decreased during this time period, and students are at greater risk of violence outside schools than within schools.

37. The description "in danger of failing to complete their education with a level of skills necessary to survive in a modern society" best describes which of the following?
- a. Low-SES students
- b. Cultural minority students
- c. Students with ineffective learning styles
- d. Students placed at-risk

38. A new teacher was hired to teach in the inner-city schools and wanted to know what adjustments she needed to make to work with students placed at-risk. Which of the following is the most important adjustment?
- a. Allow the students to work individually, such as on worksheets and computer drill-and-practice activities.
- b. Carry the content to the students personally through interactive teaching.
- c. Expect student apathy and boredom; be prepared to maintain high levels of classroom discipline.
- d. Decrease expectations to ensure that students will be successful.

39. According to research the most effective of the following interventions for increasing the achievement of students placed at-risk is to
- a. increase the number of quizzes given.
- b. increase the number of As and Bs given.
- c. slightly relax the standards for classroom management and discipline.
- d. give the students more opportunity to respond to written materials, such as worksheets.

40. Which of the following best describes the primary criticism of the term *at-risk*?
   a. It is not linked to instructional interventions.
   b. It is antiquated and doesn't address modern concerns.
   c. It doesn't recognize the diversity found in populations of students placed at-risk .
   d. It creates lowered expectations for student success.

41. Of the following which most strongly contributes to the development of resilience?
   a. The nurturing of a caring adult
   b. A variety of experiences in the preschool years
   c. Positive identity with cultural attitudes and values
   d. An instinctive desire to succeed

42. Which of the following best describes the relationship between challenge and effective instruction for students placed at-risk?
   a. Challenge is effective for some students placed at-risk but not all.
   b. Challenge increases motivation for nearly all students placed at-risk because it emphasizes high expectations.
   c. Challenge can be overemphasized, resulting in discouragement.
   d. Challenge can be misinterpreted by many students placed at-risk.

43. Which of the following are accurate descriptions of effective instruction for students placed at-risk?
   (1) It emphasizes *how* to learn as well as *what* to learn.
   (2) It stresses the importance of student responsibility and self-regulation.
   (3) It simplifies the curriculum and makes it easier.
   (4) It provides greater structure, support, and feedback than might be provided for students not at-risk.

   a. 1, 2, 4
   b. 1, 3, 4
   c. 2, 3, 4
   d. 1, 2, 3

Items for Analysis and Critical Thinking

44. Read the following exchanges, and then select the best answer below.

"I want you in by 10:00," Ellen's dad says to her as she gets ready for her roller skating party, and then he turns back to his computer.
"Aww, Dad," Ellen protests. "The party isn't over till 11:00, and a bunch of parents will be there chaperoning." "I said 10:00."
"Gee, Dad, why?"
"Ellen, I said 10:00 on school nights."
"But, Dad, there's no school tomorrow. It's a teacher planning day."
"Ellen, I said 10:00. The discussion is over," her dad says with frustration in his voice.

"Tell me about school," Tanya's dad says to her over dinner. They talk for several minutes about school, social activities, and life in general. "Now, when is your concert? I've sort of forgotten."
"Thursday," Tanya replies.
"Oh, yeah, remind me to call George and tell him I won't be able to meet him on Thursday," he says to Tanya's mother. "Tanya's concert is that night."
They finish dinner, and her dad finally says, "Better get started with your homework."
"Aww, Dad," Tanya grumbles.
"No, get going. . . . I'm working in here, so let me know if you get stuck on any of it, and I'll try and help you. . . . I want to see it when you're finished. "

"Where's Ian?" her dad asks her mother at 9:30 Thursday evening.

"She called after school and said she was going home with Christy," her mother responded.

"Didn't she say she had a test tomorrow? . . .When is she going to study?"

"She said she was fine, and besides she's not too crazy about biology. I know her grades aren't as good as they could be, but you're only young once."

If the young people's characteristics are consistent with generalizations identified by research, the persons most likely to develop bullying behaviors is(are)
   a. Ellen.
   b. Tanya.
   c. Ian.
   d. Tanya and Ian.

45. You observe that Jerome, a homosexual student in your class, is being repeatedly harassed by Calvin and David, two other boys in your class. Of the following which is your most appropriate response?
   a. Since Jerome isn't being physically harmed, ignore the incidents because students should learn to work problems out for themselves.
   b. Take Calvin and David aside and tell them that you realize that their behavior is in fun but that you believe it is hurting Jerome's feelings, and ask them how they would feel if they were being teased.
   c. Take Calvin and David aside and tell them that you have a zero tolerance policy for harassment and that one more incident of harassment will result in severe consequences.
   d. Talk to Jerome and tell him that you will support any form of retaliation that he directs toward Calvin and David.

Use the following information for Items 46 and 47:

You notice that Katrina, one of your higher-achieving eighth graders, has abruptly begun doing slipshod work. She hasn't turned in your last three assignments, and she failed your latest test. She also seems very withdrawn in learning activities, giving one-word, barely audible answers when you call on her. Always a well-groomed girl, she has begun coming to school looking disheveled and unkempt.

46. Of the following what is the best assessment of your observations of Katrina?
   a. She has become sexually active, and her interest in school and school activities has declined as a result.
   b. She has begun using hard drugs (such as cocaine), and the drug use has decreased her interest in school.
   c. She is displaying indicators of potential suicide, and her loss of interest in school and life itself are the result.
   d. She is displaying the symptoms of sexual harassment, and as a result she is withdrawing from school-related activities.

47. Of the following what is your most appropriate action in working with Katrina?
   a. Continue to watch her closely to see if her former patterns of behavior return.
   b. Talk to her and remind her that she must begin studying and turning in her work, or her grades will suffer. Offer to accept the missing assignments.
   c. Contact a school counselor or school psychologist immediately, explain the changes you've seen in Katrina's behavior, and seek advice.
   d. Talk to one of her classmates, and ask if he or she knows of any problems that Katrina might be experiencing. Remind that classmate that anything said will be held in confidence.

48. You notice that Joanne, one of your second graders, frequently comes to school disheveled and with bruises on her arms. When you ask her what caused the bruises, she says that she keeps falling from her bike. Suspecting child abuse, you report what you've seen to school authorities. After an investigation, it turns out that Joanne has told the truth, and the bruises were indeed the result of falling from her bike. Furious over the allegation of child abuse, the parents file a lawsuit against you and the school. Of the following which is the most accurate assessment of your situation?

    a. You are not protected from liability since you mistakenly alleged that the parents abused Joanne.

    b. You are not protected from liability since the only evidence of child abuse was Joanne's disheveled appearance and bruises on her arms.

    c. Because of the seriousness of child abuse, teachers are often protected from liability if they can prove their claims.

    d. You are protected from liability since you honestly reported the allegation based on her disheveled appearance and bruises.

Use the following information for Items 49 and 50:

Ariel Nagales, a seventh grader, is an immigrant from the Dominican Republic. He struggles with English but is improving rapidly. He says that his family practices speaking English at the dinner table each evening. His father makes $44,000 a year as a foreman on one of the shifts at a local oil refinery. Ariel's mother stays at home since he has a sister in the second grade and a brother in kindergarten and his mother has to pick Ariel up from soccer practice each evening. He is a star on the junior high team.

    Latisha Brown, an African American student and also a seventh grader, lives with her single mother who has a full-time job working for a maid service. Latisha helps with cooking and housekeeping at home since her mother is usually exhausted when she comes home and Latisha has a younger brother and two younger sisters. She usually finishes the housework by 8 pm, and then finishes her homework while her mother helps her brother and sisters with their school assignments. "It's sometimes hard," Latisha laments, "because I'm tired on the days that I have choir practice, but it's worth it. I have a solo part in the next concert."

    Henry Martinez comes to your class a month after school began. You check Henry's background and find that his parents were divorced shortly after they immigrated to this country from the Philippines. Henry lives with his mother, who is transferred regularly in her job as a government liaison for federal minority programs. Henry has attended four different schools in the last 3 years. In a letter to the school, Mrs. Martinez expresses concern over the frequent moves but says she can't afford to give up her $40,000 a year job. She also proudly points out that Henry was an all-star on his youth soccer team at the last school he attended. Henry speaks of her and his two younger sisters often, frequently citing examples of some of the fun things they have done together on the weekends and the interesting stories his mother reads to them in the evenings.

    Calvin Henry, another African American seventh grader, lives in Brentwood, a local inner-city area. Calvin has been living with his grandmother, an energetic 65-year-old, since his parents' divorce 4 years ago. They struggle to make ends meet since his grandmother's only source of income is social security. Calvin is both athletic and musical, and his grandmother continually encourages him to begin playing a musical instrument and go out for the junior high track team. "You would be a star," she smiles. Calvin shrugs and says maybe when he gets into high school. Right now he would rather hang out with his friends after school.

49. If the students fit patterns identified by research, the student who has the *greatest* likelihood of being placed at-risk is

    a. Ariel.

    b. Latisha.

    c. Henry.

    d. Calvin.

50. If the students fit patterns identified by research, the student who has the *least* likelihood of being placed at-risk is

    a. Ariel.

    b. Latisha.

    c. Henry.

    d. Calvin.

Extended-Response Items

51. Describe two important changes in the American family. Describe the implications that these changes have for you as a teacher. (4 points)

52. Describe three ways in which socioeconomic status can influence student learning. In your description compare patterns in high-SES families to patterns that tend to exist in low-SES families. (6 points)

53. Describe your legal obligation in cases of suspected child abuse. Also describe your legal liability. (4 points)

54. Describe three criticisms of zero tolerance policies that lead to school suspensions. Explain the criticism in each case. (6 points)

55. Describe what your primary teaching problems will be in your day-to-day work with students. Also describe the likelihood of an incident of violence occurring in your classroom. (4 points)

56. Look again at Henry Martinez (part of the information used for Items 49 and 50).

Henry Martinez comes to your class a month after school began. You check Henry's background and find that his parents were divorced shortly after they immigrated to this country from the Philippines. Henry lives with his mother, who is transferred regularly in her job as a government liaison for federal minority programs. Henry has attended four different schools in the last 3 years. In a letter to the school, Mrs. Martinez expresses concern over the frequent moves but says she can't afford to give up her $40,000 a year job. She also proudly points out that Henry was an all-star on his youth soccer team at the last school he attended. Henry speaks of her and his two younger sisters often, frequently citing examples of some of the fun things they have done together on the weekends and the interesting stories his mother reads to them in the evenings.

Identify two characteristics that would make Henry a student placed at-risk. Then identify two other characteristics that counteract Henry's being placed at-risk. (4 points)

CHAPTER FIVE

EDUCATION IN THE UNITED STATES: ITS HISTORICAL ROOTS

Knowledge-Level Items

1. The historical period in American education that most contributed to the strong link between religion and education, which remains today, was the
   - a. colonial period.
   - b. early national period.
   - c. common school movement.
   - d. Progressive Era.

2. Schooling during the colonial period was designed primarily for which of the following groups?
   - a. Wealthy males
   - b. Males of all socioeconomic classes
   - c. Wealthy males and wealthy females
   - d. Males of all socioeconomic classes and wealthy females

3. Although religion was an important influence in all the colonies—northern, middle, and southern—during the colonial period, it was the most dominant influence in the
   - a. northern colonies.
   - b. middle colonies.
   - c. southern colonies.

4. Which of the following is the best definition of *vouchers*?
   - a. Financial aid to parents of low-SES families that can be used to help them meet basic needs, such as free or reduced lunch for students
   - b. Financial aid for schools to support supplementary programs for bilingual students
   - c. Financial supplements that parents can use to purchase education at a school of their choice
   - d. Block grants to schools that can be used to purchase educational support, such as technology

5. Which of the following describes the relationship between character education and religion during the colonial period?
   - a. Character education and religion were separated because of the principle of separation of church and state.
   - b. Character education and religious training were two different approaches to moral development of colonial students.
   - c. Character education was one of the basic parts of the curriculum—together with reading, math, and science—in colonial education.
   - d. Character education and religion were synonymous in colonial education.

6. Of the following which is the most accurate description of the significance of the Massachusetts Act of 1647 (the "Old Deluder Satan Act")?
   - a. It provided the precedent for the principle of separation of church and state.
   - b. It provided a legal foundation for the public support of education.
   - c. It provided a framework for differentiating American education from its European roots.
   - d. It made public education mandatory for all children aged 5 to 13.

7. Of the following which is most significant about the colonial period in helping us understand American education today?
   - a. It helps us understand why teacher preparation programs (such as the one you're in) came to exist.
   - b. It helps us understand why the federal government has turned much of the responsibility for education over to the states.
   - c. It helps us understand how the present organization of elementary, middle, and high schools came to exist.
   - d. It helps us understand why religion remains an important issue in American education.

8. Which of the following is the best description of *character education?*
   a.   An approach to developing character traits that exists in private religious schools but not in public schools
   b.   An approach to the development of moral reasoning that focuses on case studies of moral issues
   c.   An approach to developing morals in students that emphasizes the transmission of moral values, such as honesty, into character traits
   d.   An approach to education in which each person is asked to reflect on his or her character traits and make decisions about how he or she might become a better citizen

9. Of the following the two most significant contributions of the early national period (1775–1820) that remain today were
   a.   establishment of public support for education and the development of the comprehensive high school.
   b.   the separation of church and state and the removal of the federal government from a central role in running America's schools.
   c.   the establishment of the Department of Education as a federal cabinet post and the creation of vouchers to support religion for all free members of society.
   d.   the "Old Deluder Satan Act" and the establishment of a widespread system of parochial schools.

10. The leaders that framed the American Constitution refused to establish a national religion in the United States. Which of the following is the best description of the reason for the leaders' refusal?
   a.   The leaders were afraid that a national religion might lead to the kind of religious persecution that existed in Europe.
   b.   The leaders adopted the principle of separation of church and state that had been established in England during the 1600s.
   c.   The leaders recognized that a great deal of religious diversity existed in the colonies, making the establishment of a national religion very difficult.
   d.   The leaders wanted to eliminate the influence of religion in America, and they believed that the refusal to establish a national religion would help them reach that goal.

11. Which of the following statements best describes the contribution of the Northwest Ordinance of 1785 to education in America?
   a.   It was the law that formally established the principle of separation of church and state.
   b.   It was the law that removed the federal government from direct involvement in running America's schools.
   c.   It was the law that established free public education for all students.
   d.   It was the law that set aside land that would be used to financially support public education.

12. Which of the following best describes the legal action that resulted in every state in the United States now having its own office of education?
   a.   The First Amendment to the Constitution, which established the principle of separation of church and state
   b.   The Northwest Ordinance of 1785, which provided a basis for financial support of education
   c.   The Tenth Amendment to the Constitution, which said that areas not assigned to the federal government would be the responsibilities of the states
   d.   The Old Deluder Satan Act, which provided for public support of education

13. Of the following which is the best description of the Common School Movement?
   a.   A historical attempt to make education available to all children in the United States
   b.   An attempt to increase the quality of teachers by establishing normal schools
   c.   The process of reserving public land specifically for the purpose of funding public education
   d.   The process of putting common people in leadership roles in education

14. Which of the following statements best describes the contribution Horace Mann made to American education?
    a. He spearheaded legislation that led to the principle of separation of church and state.
    b. He spearheaded the idea that all citizens should have the right to attend a tax-supported elementary school.
    c. He was the leader of the movement to remove the federal government from direct involvement in running America's schools.
    d. He was the person who wrote and spearheaded the passing of the Northwest Ordinance of 1785.

15. Which of the following contributed to the idea that free public education should be the right of all citizens?
    (1) The principle of separation of church and state
    (2) The increasing industrialization of the United States during the approximate period between 1820 and 1865
    (3) The large influx of immigrants from Europe and other parts of the world that began in about the 1830s
    (4) The Northwest Ordinance of 1785 which established an economic basis for public education

    a. 1, 2, 3, 4
    b. 1, 4
    c. 1, 3, 4
    d. 2, 3

16. Which of the following is the best description of *normal schools*?
    a. Schools designed to educate all members of society, not just the elite
    b. Schools designed to focus on secular more than religious education
    c. Schools designed to prepare young men for careers in law or the ministry
    d. Schools designed to prepare prospective teachers for America's schools

17. Which of the following most contributed to the increase in quality of America's schools during the period from approximately 1820 to 1865?
    a. Improvement in teacher preparation and the introduction of grade levels in elementary schools
    b. The Northwest Ordinance of 1785 and the establishment of the comprehensive high school
    c. The practice of using people preparing for the ministry as teachers and the establishment of middle schools
    d. Tax support for public schools and control of education being given to the states

18. Of the following which best describes an important problem with tax support for public schools?
    a. Citizens are reluctant to pay school taxes, so adequate funding sometimes isn't available.
    b. Funding is often inequitable because some districts have high tax bases, whereas others have very low tax bases.
    c. Most of the taxes are paid by wealthy people who are unwilling to support education for all citizens.
    d. Only a small portion of tax money goes to education, so education is consistently underfunded.

19. Approximately what percent of all students attended high school at the beginning of the twentieth century?
    a. Less than 10 percent
    b. About 25 percent
    c. About 50 percent
    d. About 75 percent

Use the following information for Items 20–22:

Although the comprehensive American high school wasn't well established until the twentieth century, its roots go back to the Latin grammar school established in 1635; Benjamin Franklin's academy, which first opened in 1751; and the English classical school (later changed to the English high school), which opened in 1821.

20. Which of the following best describes the goal of the Latin grammar school?
    a. To prepare students for law and the ministry
    b. To help students develop practical skills, such as math, navigation, bookkeeping, and logic
    c. To help some students develop practical job skills and others prepare for college
    d. To help students acquire basic skills, such as reading, writing, and math

21. Which of the following best describes the goal of Franklin's academy?
    a. To prepare students for law and the ministry
    b. To help students develop practical skills, such as math, navigation, bookkeeping, and logic
    c. To help some students develop practical job skills and others prepare for college
    d. To help students acquire basic skills, such as reading, writing, and math

22. Of the Latin grammar school, Franklin's academy, the English high school, and the comprehensive high school, which two are most alike?
    a. The Latin grammar school and the English high school
    b. The Latin grammar school and Franklin's academy
    c. Franklin's academy and the English high school
    d. The English high school and the comprehensive high school

23. Which of the following best describes *faculty psychology*?
    a. A view of learning that suggests that students learn best when taught by well-prepared teachers
    b. A view of learning that emphasizes the role of experience and hands-on activities in learning
    c. A view of learning suggesting that the best education involves mental discipline and training the powers of the mind
    d. A view of learning that emphasizes a study of classic literature, such as Shakespeare, which has endured throughout history

24. Of the following what are reasons that the Committee of Ten recommended that all students—both college bound and non-college bound—meet the same high school requirements?
   (1) The committee was composed of college professors and administrators, who had a bias in favor of a college preparatory curriculum.
   (2) The committee believed in the need for basic skills—reading, writing, and math—that all students should master.
   (3) The members of the committee believed in faculty psychology, which emphasized mental training for all students.
   (4) The members of the committee believed that a different curriculum for college-bound and non-college-bound students might result in separation of social classes.

    a. 1, 2, 3, 4
    b. 1, 3, 4
    c. 2, 3, 4
    d. 2, 4

25. Of the following which event most led to the development of the American high school as we know it today?
    a. The development of the English high school, whose curriculum included English, math, science, history, and geography
    b. The preparation of the report titled "The Cardinal Principles of Education," which established goals for high schools
    c. The establishment of normal schools, which resulted in a teaching force able to work effectively in modern high schools
    d. The establishment of different grades in elementary schools, which better prepared students for the rigorous content of high schools

26. Of the following which is the most likely reason that progressive education declined after the middle of the twentieth century?
    a. The content of the progressive education curriculum was criticized as not being relevant to the lives of students.
    b. Progressive education was very costly to implement and maintain, and the excessive costs eventually caused it to decline in prominence.
    c. Teaching according to the progressive education philosophy required a great deal of professional development for teachers, which school districts were unable to provide.
    d. Critics denounced "life adjustment" features of progressive education as watered down and devoid of content and intellectual rigor.

27. The progressive education movement has left two important questions unanswered. Which of the following best identifies these questions?
    a. Which students should participate in college-bound tracks, and which students should be in technical tracks?
    b. What curriculum content is most valuable, and how should that content be taught?
    c. How can schools best accommodate cultural diversity, and how should schools respond to gender differences?
    d. When should curriculum be integrated, and how should curriculum integration be accomplished?

28. The educational movement that attempted to bring cultural minorities into mainstream American life by teaching basic skills and white middle-class values is best described as
    a. separate but equal.
    b. progressive education.
    c. assimilation.
    d. mainstreaming.

29. The assimilation movement in education was most strongly attempted with
    a. Native American students.
    b. African American students.
    c. Hispanic students.
    d. Asian American students.

30. The policy separate but equal in education was most prominently implemented in
    a. Native American education.
    b. African American education.
    c. Hispanic education.
    d. Asian American education.

31. The cultural minorities with the highest school dropout rates are
    a. Native American students.
    b. African American students.
    c. Hispanic students.
    d. Asian American students.

32. The cultural minorities who have experienced the greatest success in American schools are
    a. Native American students.
    b. African American students.
    c. Hispanic students.
    d. Asian American students.

33. Of the following which is most commonly cited as an important reason for the lack of success of Hispanic students?
    a.   The lack of motivation of many Hispanic students
    b.   Language differences that symbolize the differences between Hispanics and the dominant culture
    c.   Differences between the learning styles of most Hispanic students and the patterns of instruction found in most American schools
    d.   Antagonism between Hispanic students and other cultural minorities that results in Hispanic students being isolated from the rest of the school population

34. The event of the Cold War period that had the most important implications for education was
    a.   the Berlin airlift that resulted from the Communist blockade of Berlin.
    b.   the Korean War and the Domino Theory.
    c.   the Soviet launching of Sputnik.
    d.   the Cuban missile crisis that nearly caused World War III.

35. Which of the following is the most important result of Russia's launching of Sputnik in 1957?
    a.   It resulted in a dramatic increase in funding for math, science, and teacher training.
    b.   It precipitated the progressive education movement, which made the school curriculum much more relevant to students' lives.
    c.   It resulted in a standardized high school curriculum that raised the standards for the education of all students.
    d.   It precipitated the modern reform movement that emphasized standards-based education and school accountability.

36. "A federal compensatory preschool education program designed to help 3- and 4-year-old disadvantaged students enter school ready to learn" is most accurately labeled
    a.   Head Start.
    b.   Title I.
    c.   Progressive Education.
    d.   Individuals with Disabilities Education Act.

37. "A federal compensatory education program targeting low-income students in elementary and secondary schools" is most accurately labeled
    a.   Head Start.
    b.   Title I.
    c.   National Defense Education Act.
    d.   Individuals with Disabilities Education Act.

38. The Supreme Court decision that made the policy separate but equal illegal was
    a.   the Civil Rights Act.
    b.   the *Brown v. Board of Education of Topeka* decision.
    c.   Title IX.
    d.   the National Defense Education Act.

39. The legislation intended to eliminate gender bias in schools was
    a.   Title IX.
    b.   PL 94–142.
    c.   the Gender Equity Legislative Mandate.
    d.   the Civil Rights Act.

40. Schools that attempt to attract African American and white students through quality instruction or innovative programs are most accurately labeled
    a.   progressive schools.
    b.   Title I schools.
    c.   integrated schools.
    d.   magnet schools.

Items for Analysis and Critical Thinking

41. Consider the schools in the southern colonies—Maryland, Virginia, the Carolinas, and Georgia—during the colonial period. Which of the following statements is most valid?
    a.   The colonies were religiously diverse, so each colony created parochial schools for the children of the colony.
    b.   Because many people lived on plantations that were long distances from each other, parents hired tutors to educate their children.
    c.   Because many people lived and worked in agriculture, education was more egalitarian than in the middle and northern colonies.
    d.   Education focused primarily on religious training, which was grounded in the belief that humanity was evil by its nature, having fallen in the sin of Adam and Eve.

42. Consider the schools in the middle colonies—New York, New Jersey, Delaware, and Pennsylvania—during the colonial period. Which of the following statements is most valid?
    a.   The colonies were religiously diverse, so each colony created parochial schools for the children of the colony.
    b.   Because many people worked in towns that had industry and commerce, families collaborated to hire tutors for several families' children.
    c.   Because many people came from working class—instead of aristocratic—backgrounds, education was more egalitarian than in the northern and southern colonies.
    d.   Education focused primarily on religious training, which was grounded in the belief that humanity was evil by its nature, having fallen in the sin of Adam and Eve.

43. Consider the schools in the New England colonies—Massachusetts, Connecticut, and New Hampshire—during the colonial period. Which of the following statements is most valid?
    a.   The colonies were religiously diverse, so each colony created parochial schools for the children of the colony.
    b.   Because many people worked in towns that had industry and commerce, families collaborated to hire tutors for several families' children.
    c.   Because many people came from working class, rather than aristocratic, backgrounds, education was more egalitarian than in the middle and southern colonies.
    d.   Education focused primarily on religious training, which was grounded in the belief that humanity was evil by its nature, having fallen in the sin of Adam and Eve.

44. Which of the following statements best describes the significance of the Old Deluder Satan Act (the Massachusetts Act of 1647), which was designed to create citizens that were literate with respect to the Bible?
    a.   It established a link between education and religion in the southern states—such as Alabama, Mississippi, and Louisiana—that remains today.
    b.   It set a precedent for controversies surrounding religion that led to the principle of separation of church and state.
    c.   It provided the legal foundation for public support of education.
    d.   It established a precedent that led to the widespread system of parochial schools that exists in the United States today.

45. During the colonial period of American education, the thinking of some European philosophers—such as Locke, Rousseau, and Pestalozzi—began to influence education. Of the following which is the most accurate description of their influence?
    a.   These philosophers emphasized memorization and recitation as training for the mind.
    b.   These philosophers emphasized the importance of first-hand experiences for children as the foundation for their education.
    c.   These philosophers emphasized education for all citizens instead of reserving education for the wealthy elite.
    d.   These philosophers emphasized differences between religion and education that contributed to establishing the principle of separation of church and state.

46. Janet, a math teacher; Cal, who teaches American history; Lamont, an English teacher; and Karen, a science teacher are meeting during their common planning period to discuss some students who appear to be having problems in each of their classes. They also are working on integrating their curriculum. Lamont agrees to have his class begin reading *Uncle Tom's Cabin* since Cal's students are studying the American Civil War and the publication of the book was one of the factors that precipitated the war. Their discussion then continues. Based on this information, it most likely that these teachers teach in a(n)

    a.   elementary school.
    b.   middle school.
    c.   junior high.
    d.   high school.

47. Of the following which example best illustrates a learning activity based on progressive education ideas?

    a.   Jack Manning carefully explains the concept of *camouflage*. After explaining the concept, he shows the students colored slides of a snake camouflaged in some grass and an insect camouflaged on a leaf.
    b.   Molly Miller puts students into groups of three, and each group reads a section of their textbook that describes how animals protect themselves, with camouflage being one of the ways. The groups each then report back to the whole class.
    c.   Ashley Wilson takes boxes of red, green, yellow, and blue toothpicks and randomly distributes them on a section of the school grounds. She then takes the students outside and gives them 5 minutes to collect as many toothpicks as they can find. They discuss reasons that they found different numbers of each color.
    d.   Ken Davis has his students search the Internet for information on camouflage. The students find articles and research reports, print them, and then make oral reports to the class about the information they've gathered.

Extended-Response Items

48. Describe the cultural and economic differences in the southern, middle, and northern colonies during the colonial period, and explain how the types of schools that were created were the result of these differences. (6 points)

49. Each of the important historical periods in the history of American education—the colonial period (1607–1775), the early national period (1775–1820), and the common school movement (1820–1865)—left an important legacy that remains today. Identify and explain the most important legacy left by each of these historical periods.

50. Explain the assimilation movement in education in detail. Assess its success, and provide evidence for your assessment. (6 points)

51. Describe the differences between Booker T. Washington's and W.E.B. Dubois' suggestions for improving the education of African Americans. Describe differences in their personal backgrounds that could have contributed to their views. (4 points)

52. Using research as a basis, write an assessment of the success of Head Start and Title I. Carefully explain the success (or lack of success) in each case. (4 points)

53. Describe the controversies that exist with respect to civil rights and equity for women. Cite arguments for both sides of the issues in describing the controversies. (4 points)

CHAPTER SIX

EDUCATIONAL PHILOSOPHY: THE INTELLECTUAL FOUNDATIONS OF AMERICAN EDUCATION

Knowledge-Level Items

1. At a most basic level, philosophy is often described as
   a. a search for wisdom.
   b. a set of fundamental principles.
   c. a guide for action in our daily lives.
   d. a system of beliefs about how the world works.

2. Which of the following best states a formal description of philosophy?
   a. The study of the universe and the place of humanity within it
   b. The study of the moral principles of truth, justice, and honor
   c. The study of the big questions in life, such as the origin and the end of the universe
   d. The study of theories of knowledge, truth, existence, and good

3. "A framework for thinking about educational issues and a guide for professional practice" best describes which of the following?
   a. An epistemology of education
   b. An ontology of education
   c. An axiology of education
   d. A philosophy of education

4. Which of the following best states the role of philosophy in teacher professionalism?
   a. It helps ensure that professional teachers will be ethical in their dealings with students.
   b. It is an essential part of the knowledge base teachers use to make decisions.
   c. It is an essential part of teachers' classroom strategies.
   d. It ensures that students who are members of cultural minorities will be instructed without cultural bias.

5. Which of the following statements best describes the relationship between theory and philosophy?
   a. Theories explain observations in the world, and philosophy explains people's thoughts and emotions.
   b. Philosophy is used to analyze ideas, but theories go beyond philosophy to explain observations and events.
   c. Theories explain observations in the world, but philosophy goes beyond theory to describe how things ought to be.
   d. Theories are based on principles, and philosophy is used to form the principles.

6. A description of the way education, architecture, and any other profession ought to practice is called
   a. professional theory.
   b. normative philosophy.
   c. character education.
   d. values clarification.

7. Which of the following is *not* a branch of philosophy?
   a. Paleontology
   b. Epistemology
   c. Ontology
   d. Axiology

8. The branch of philosophy that deals with questions of *how* we come to know what we know is
   a. axiology.
   b. ontology.
   c. epistemology.
   d. ethics.

9. "We're never sure an idea is true until it's tested with factual evidence" is a statement that reflects
   a. epistemology.
   b. ontology.
   c. axiology.
   d. logic.

10. The branch of philosophy that considers the nature of reality is
   a. epistemology.
   b. ontology.
   c. axiology.
   d. logic.

11. The branch of philosophy that considers values and ethics is
   a. epistemology.
   b. ontology.
   c. psychology.
   d. axiology.

12. The debate between *character education*, a view suggesting that values such as honesty should be emphasized, taught, and rewarded, and *moral education*, a view emphasizing the development of moral reasoning, most closely relates to
   a. epistemology.
   b. ontology.
   c. axiology.
   d. logic.

13. One person argues that reality is objective and observable, and another argues that reality is actually perceived since our behavior depends on our perceptions. This debate is most closely related to
   a. epistemology.
   b. ontology.
   c. axiology.
   d. logic.

14. A teacher who says, "I'm getting paid to help kids learn, and I'm not earning my salary if I don't give it my very best" is making a statement most closely related to
   a. epistemology.
   b. ontology.
   c. axiology.
   d. logic.

15. The statement "the physical world is constantly changing, so ideas are the only reliable form of reality" best describes
   a. idealism.
   b. realism.
   c. pragmatism.
   d. existentialism.

16. The argument that "a real world exists regardless of whether or not a human being is there to perceive it" best describes
   a. idealism.
   b. realism.
   c. pragmatism.
   d. existentialism.

17. Which traditional philosophy rejects the idea of absolute, unchanging truth?
   a. Idealism
   b. Realism
   c. Pragmatism
   d. Existentialism

18. Which traditional philosophy is based on the view that humanity isn't part of an orderly universe and that individuals create their own realities in their own unique ways?
   a. Idealism
   b. Realism
   c. Pragmatism
   d. Existentialism

19. Of the traditional philosophies the one that would advocate the most learner-centered curriculum and instruction would most likely be
   a. idealism.
   b. realism.
   c. pragmatism.
   d. existentialism.

20. Some schools strongly emphasize basic skills, such as reading, writing, math, and perhaps now computer literacy. The educational philosophy most closely associated with this emphasis is
   a. perennialism.
   b. essentialism.
   c. progressivism.
   d. postmodernism.

21. Reforms aimed at improving teacher training have emphasized that teachers have stronger backgrounds in the content areas in which they'll be teaching (such as people preparing to be math teachers having stronger backgrounds in math). This position is most strongly grounded in
   a. perennialism.
   b. essentialism.
   c. progressivism.
   d. postmodernism.

22. Which of the following statements best describes the primary difference between perennialism and essentialism?
   a. Essentialism is more strongly grounded in idealism and realism than is perennialism.
   b. Essentialism more strongly emphasizes the importance of knowledge and skills that are useful in today's world than does perennialism.
   c. Essentialism emphasizes learner-centered instruction, whereas perennialism emphasizes teacher-centered instruction.
   d. Essentialism emphasizes epistemology (how we know), whereas perennialism emphasizes ontology (what we know).

23. A teacher who believes that students are best educated when they study the ideas that have endured through history, such as math, science, and great literature, is most strongly guided by
   a. perennialism.
   b. essentialism.
   c. progressivism.
   d. postmodernism.

24. Which of the following statements best describes essentialists' and perennialists' positions with respect to learner-centered instruction and the development of learner self-esteem?
   a. Both philosophies strongly emphasize learner-centered instruction, and the development of self-esteem is a primary goal for both.
   b. Essentialism strongly emphasizes learner-centered instruction and the development of self-esteem, whereas perennialism does not.
   c. Perennialism strongly emphasizes learner-centered instruction and the development of self-esteem, whereas essentialism does not.
   d. Both philosophies are very wary of learner-centered instruction, and the development of self-esteem is not a goal for either.

25. The educational philosophy emphasizing curriculum that focuses on real-world problem solving and individual development best describes
   a. perennialism.
   b. essentialism.
   c. progressivism.
   d. postmodernism.

26. Of the following what is the most commonly voiced criticism of perennialism?
   a. It is elitist and places too much emphasis on ideas that are unrelated to students' lives.
   b. It places too much emphasis on individual growth and students' self-esteem.
   c. It is too strongly influenced by an emphasis on basic skills.
   d. It is not appropriately grounded in one of the traditional philosophies.

27. Progressivism is most strongly grounded in which of the traditional philosophies?
   a. Idealism
   b. Realism
   c. Pragmatism
   d. Existentialism

28. Constructivism is a learning theory that says that learners don't behave like tape recorders, that is, they don't store information in their memories in the same form in which they heard or read it. Rather, they create understanding that makes sense to them by relating what they hear or read to what they already know, and they store in memory the understanding they have created for themselves. This view of learning is most strongly grounded in
   a. idealism and perennialism.
   b. realism and essentialism.
   c. pragmatism and progressivism.
   d. existentialism and postmodernism.

29. Of the following which is the most commonly voiced criticism of progressivism?
   a. It too strongly emphasizes content that isn't relevant to students' present-day world.
   b. It places too much emphasis on students' interest and self-esteem at the expense of understanding.
   c. It places too much emphasis on basic skills, such as reading, writing, and math, and doesn't place enough emphasis on other content areas, such as science and social studies.
   d. It is too teacher-centered, and as a result it detracts from student motivation.

30. Of the following the most commonly voiced criticism of postmodernism is that
   a. it is elitist and places too much emphasis on historical ideas irrelevant to students' lives.
   b. it has abandoned schools as places for learning, instead using schools for political purposes.
   c. it places too much emphasis on the individual and student self-esteem.
   d. it places too much emphasis on basic skills at the expense of other parts of the curriculum.

31. The explanation and rationale you provide for your educational goals—what you want to accomplish in your classroom—will most strongly depend on
    a. your personal philosophy.
    b. your personal needs.
    c. your self-esteem.
    d. your work ethic and sense of responsibility.

32. Of the following the most important factor in critically examining your beliefs is likely to be
    a. epistemology.
    b. ontology.
    c. axiology.
    d. logic.

Items for Analysis and Critical Thinking

Use the following information for Items 33 and 34:

Claire Gonzales and Antonio Rivera, two middle school teachers, are involved in a discussion. "This 'feel good' stuff has set education back 30 years," Claire asserts. "We know that people are motivated by the extent to which they expect to succeed on challenging tasks. So what we should be doing is challenging them and helping them to succeed. There is information everyone needs in order to function in today's world, and we need to hold kids' feet to the fire to be sure that they learn it."

"That's all well and good," Antonio responds, "but how do you know what knowledge is the most important for them to learn? Who is going to decide what is most important? I think kids need to learn how to get information on their own. Then they'll be better equipped to function in today's world."

33. Which of the following statements best describes Claire's comments?
    a. Her comments include explanations based on theory but not statements that reflect philosophy.
    b. Her comments include statements that reflect philosophy but not explanations that are based on theory.
    c. Her statements include both explanations based on theory and statements that reflect philosophy.
    d. Her statements reflect neither explanations based on theory nor statements that reflect philosophy.

34. Which of the following statements best describes Antonio's comments?
    a. His comments include explanations based on theory but not statements that reflect philosophy.
    b. His comments include statements that reflect philosophy but not explanations that are based on theory.
    c. His statements include both explanations based on theory and statements that reflect philosophy.
    d. His statements reflect neither explanations based on theory nor statements that reflect philosophy.

35. A person decides that Japanese-built cars are more reliable than American-built cars, saying he looked in a consumer rating magazine that cited the average incidents of repair for Toyotas, Nissans, Hondas, Chevrolets, Fords, and Chryslers. Which of the following best describes his decision?
    a. It is primarily based on deductive reasoning.
    b. It is primarily based on inductive reasoning.
    c. It is primarily based on epistemological reasoning.
    d. It is primarily based on metaphysical reasoning.

36. Brad Gilbert believes that learners construct their own understanding of the topics they study. He provides a variety of experiences for learners and leads discussions intended to help them construct valid understandings of the way the world works. Ann Wilson believes that authority is the most important way of knowing, and she presents carefully organized lectures that cover the topics she wants her students to understand. The differences in the two teachers' beliefs are most nearly suggested by which of the following?
    a. Ethics
    b. Ontology
    c. Axiology
    d. Epistemology

Use the following information for Items 37–40:

"I'm eating too much," Jennifer complains. "How do you know?" Louanne wonders. "When you take in more calories than you burn, you gain weight, and I've gained 5 pounds in the last 6 months," Jennifer responds.

37. Jennifer's statement "I'm eating too much" is best described as a
     a. major premise.
     b. minor premise.
     c. conclusion.
     d. result of inductive reasoning.

38. Jennifer's statement "When you take in more calories than you burn, you gain weight" is best described as a
     a. major premise.
     b. minor premise.
     c. conclusion.
     d. result of deductive reasoning.

39. Jennifer's statement "I've gained 5 pounds in the last 6 months" is best described as a
     a. major premise.
     b. minor premise.
     c. conclusion.
     d. result of deductive reasoning.

40. Jennifer's comments are best described as
     a. deductive reasoning but not inductive reasoning.
     b. inductive reasoning but not deductive reasoning.
     c. both inductive and deductive reasoning.
     d. both inductive and epistemological reasoning.

41. A teacher has her seventh graders study the novel *The Yearling* because she believes students should examine moral dilemmas, which have existed throughout history. This teacher's philosophy is most likely to be
     a. idealism.
     b. postmodernism.
     c. pragmatism.
     d. existentialism.

42. Davis Elementary School places particular emphasis on reading, writing, math, and science because "if the kids become good in these areas, they have the tools needed to understand the world around them." The philosophy of Davis Elementary School is most likely grounded in
     a. progressivism.
     b. realism.
     c. pragmatism.
     d. existentialism.

43. Juan Nagales is a strong proponent of problem-based learning, an approach to instruction in which students are given an ill-defined, real-world problem that requires an extended period of time to solve. As the students work, Juan provides only enough guidance to keep the students from going too far down blind alleys and wasting time. Juan's philosophy is most likely grounded in
     a. idealism.
     b. realism.
     c. pragmatism.
     d. existentialism.

44. Karen Ravitch has her fifth graders working on activities in which they determine the densities of different liquids—such as water, alcohol, cooking oil, and glycerin—by putting equal volumes on balances and seeing which ones are heavier. They also see which ones will float on others by pouring them together. "This is the only way they get to where they really understand the ideas," Karen contends. Karen's approach to science is most strongly grounded in
  a. perennialism.
  b. essentialism.
  c. progressivism.
  d. postmodernism.

45. A teacher has her students read Maya Angelou's *I Know Why the Caged Bird Sings* because she wants them to increase their sensitivity to literature written by cultural minorities. This teacher's goal is most likely grounded in
  a. perennialism.
  b. essentialism.
  c. progressivism.
  d. postmodernism.

Use the following information for Items 46 and 47:

One teacher presenting information about the New World emphasizes that Columbus's discovery of the New World was a critical point in European expansion and colonization, and it marked the beginning of modern history in North and South America. A second teacher notes that Columbus's discovery opened the Western Hemisphere but emphasizes that conquering and colonization were the Spaniards' primary goals and that Native Americans were brutalized and enslaved by the Spaniards.

46. The first teacher's orientation is most likely grounded in
  a. essentialism.
  b. progressivism.
  c. postmodernism.
  d. existentialism.

47. The second teacher's orientation is most likely grounded in
  a. perennialism.
  b. essentialism.
  c. progressivism.
  d. postmodernism.

Extended-Response Items

48. Describe the educational implications for each of the traditional philosophies—idealism, realism, pragmatism, and existentialism. Provide a specific, concrete example to illustrate each implication. (8 points)

49. Cite the most common criticisms of each of the traditional philosophies. Explain in each case. (8 points)

50. Cite the most common criticisms of each of the educational philosophies. Explain in each case. (8 points)

51. Native American, African, and Asian cultures have been described as having particular philosophical perspectives. Outline these descriptions, and then cite the sharp criticisms that have been directed at this approach to philosophy. (6 points)

52. Identify the educational goal, curriculum emphasis, and teaching methods that are most closely associated with each of the educational philosophies—perennialism, essentialism, progressivism, and postmodernism. (12 points)

53. Explain why forming a personal philosophy is important for teachers. Provide a specific, concrete example to illustrate your explanation. (6 points)

CHAPTER SEVEN

THE ORGANIZATION OF AMERICAN SCHOOLS

Knowledge-Level Items

1. "An organization with established structures and rules designed to promote certain goals" best describes a
   a. social institution.
   b. democratic institution.
   c. autocratic institution.
   d. socioeconomic institution.

2. Of the following which is a social institution?
   a. A city government
   b. A library building
   c. A school building
   d. Teachers in a school

3. From the perspective of meeting learning goals for students, which of the following is the most accurate definition of schools?
   a. Physical structures that house students during learning experiences
   b. Organizations composed of teachers, students, administrators, and support personnel
   c. Formal and informal curricula that present options for students' experiences
   d. Social institutions designed to promote students' growth and development

4. "An administrative unit within a geographical area given the responsibility for education within its borders" is best described as a
   a. school.
   b. school district.
   c. social institution.
   d. regional office.

5. Individual schools in a county are part of one or more organizational frameworks called
   a. regions.
   b. social institutions.
   c. districts.
   d. administrative units.

6. The person(s) given the ultimate responsibility for a school's operation is(are) the
   a. administrative staff.
   b. superintendent.
   c. vice principal.
   d. principal.

7. The people responsible for the day-to-day operation of schools are the
   a. teachers.
   b. administrators.
   c. school advisory councils.
   d. school boards.

8. *Support staff* best describes which of the following?
   a. Media center specialist
   b. Assistant principal
   c. Vice principal
   d. Guidance counselor

9. Of the following a *curriculum specialist* best describes which of the following?
   a.   A second-grade teacher in an elementary school
   b.   A math teacher in a junior high
   c.   An English teacher in a high school
   d.   A music teacher in an elementary school

10. Individual buildings on the perimeter of school campuses that provide additional classroom space are commonly called
    a.   support spaces.
    b.   temporaries.
    c.   laboratories.
    d.   extracurricular housing.

11. You're a high school math teacher. Which of the following best describes your duties?
    (1) Teach your math classes as effectively as possible.
    (2) Monitor students as they move through hallways and attend assemblies in auditoriums.
    (3) Contribute to the governance of the school.
    (4) Attend football games and other sporting events.

    a.   1
    b.   1, 2
    c.   1, 2, 3
    d.   1, 2, 3, 4

12. You're a third-grade teacher. Which of the following best describes your duties?
    (1) Teach your students as effectively as possible.
    (2) Escort your students from your room to places such as the cafeteria or media center and back.
    (3) Attend school functions, such as plays and music events.
    (4) Participate in school governance.

    a.   1
    b.   1, 2
    c.   1, 2, 3
    d.   1, 2, 4

13. "What teachers teach and what students (hopefully) learn" best describes
    a.   the school's mission.
    b.   the school's implementation process.
    c.   the school's curriculum.
    d.   the school's staff development.

14. Of the following, leaders' decisions about organizing schools (such as organizing middle schools into grades 6, 7, and 8 are most commonly based on
    a.   the backgrounds of teachers and their teaching skills.
    b.   the developmental characteristics of students and economics (such as the cost of schools).
    c.   the number of available administrators and the number of available teachers.
    d.   the qualifications of administrators and the qualifications of teachers.

15. Changes, caused by maturation and experience in the way students think and relate to their peers, are best described as
    a.   critical thinking.
    b.   development.
    c.   perspective taking.
    d.   curriculum organization.

16. Of the following which is most commonly emphasized in developmental early childhood programs?
    a. Careful curriculum organization and clear explanations by teachers
    b. Specific sets of learning objectives together with learning activities designed to help students reach the objectives
    c. Concrete experiences for students that emphasize exploration and hands-on activities
    d. Classrooms in which teachers are well prepared in content areas such as math or social studies

17. Of the following which is the most likely reason that elementary schools are organized so that many of the classrooms are self-contained (a single teacher being responsible for all the content areas)?
    a. Self-contained classrooms make integrating the curriculum most efficient, and the curriculum is usually integrated in elementary schools.
    b. Self-contained classrooms make it easier for schools to hire teachers since elementary teachers are expert in all content areas.
    c. Schools with self-contained classrooms are less expensive than schools organized around different curriculum areas.
    d. Self-contained classrooms best allow schools and teachers to accommodate the developmental needs of young children.

18. Of the following what is the best description of *looping*?
    a. The process of keeping a teacher with a group of students for more than a year
    b. The process of covering topics with increasingly greater depth from one year to the next
    c. The process of organizing curriculum so that topics build on each other
    d. The process of having teachers specialize in different content areas, such as math, science, social studies, or language arts

19. Of the following which is the most likely reason that some content areas, such as science, are typically de-emphasized in elementary schools?
    a. Elementary teachers are often uncomfortable teaching all the content areas, so some, such as science, are de-emphasized.
    b. Some content areas, such as science, are viewed as unimportant for elementary students, so they're de-emphasized.
    c. The developmental characteristics of young children prevent them from being able to learn some content areas, such as science, in depth, so they're de-emphasized.
    d. Teaching some content areas, such as science, is very expensive, so schools de-emphasize these areas.

20. Of the following which is the best description of a *comprehensive high school*?
    a. One that teaches as much of its content as possible at the comprehension level of understanding
    b. One that is designed to meet the needs of all students
    c. One that avoids tracking students in different ability areas
    d. One that has a course-sharing arrangement with a local university

21. Of the following which are the most commonly voiced criticisms of comprehensive high schools?
    (1) They're often staffed by unqualified teachers.
    (2) Students in lower-level tracks often get a substandard education.
    (3) They're too large, impersonal, and bureaucratic.
    (4) They lack an adequate variety of extracurricular activities.

    a. 1
    b. 1, 4
    c. 1, 2, 3
    d. 2, 3

22. Schools tend to be organized in box-like structures, with separate classrooms that open into long hallways. Of the following which is the most commonly voiced criticism of this physical organization?
   a. The organization makes it difficult for students to move efficiently from one room to another.
   b. The organization is dangerous since large numbers of students are moving through hallways at the same time.
   c. The organization isolates teachers and fragments the curriculum.
   d. The organization makes it difficult for administrators to communicate with individual teachers in case of emergency.

23. Which of the following statements best describes the implications of the physical organization of schools (the fact that schools are organized into individual classrooms that open onto long hallways) for you as a teacher?
   a. When you begin teaching, you're essentially on your own; you're responsible for your students all day long every day, for example.
   b. In cases of emergency you'll need to understand the physical layout of the school so that you can get help for students as quickly as possible.
   c. You'll need to understand how the physical organization of the school aids the efficient movement of students from one part of the school building to another.
   d. You'll need to understand how the arrangement of classrooms allows you to access resource rooms, such as the library and computer lab.

24. Schools are typically organized so that early elementary students, such as first graders, aren't housed in schools that also include eighth graders. Of the following the most likely reason for organizing schools in this way is
   a. the developmental differences between first and eighth graders make housing them in different schools important.
   b. schools built for young children (such as first graders) need to be designed with more safety and health-related equipment than schools designed for older students.
   c. elementary schools have fundamentally different kinds of administrators than do middle and high schools.
   d. first and eighth graders were housed in separate schools in early colonial times, and the tradition remains to this day.

25. Middle schools often eliminate activities such as competitive sports. Of the following the most likely reason for organizing middle schools in this way is
   a. school leaders want to minimize attention to developmental differences among students.
   b. school leaders don't want to spend the money it takes to support activities like competitive sports.
   c. school leaders have difficulty hiring faculty for middle schools who are willing to perform extra duties, such as coaching competitive sports.
   d. school leaders believe that the primary focus in the middle years should be on academics, so other aspects of schooling are de-emphasized in these schools.

26. Which of the following best describes classes that allow students to earn college credit while still in high school?
   a. Academic classes
   b. Honors classes
   c. Advanced placement classes
   d. Accelerated and enriched classes

27. Based on research, which of the following statements best describes the relationship between socioeconomic status, learning, and school size?
   a. All students, regardless of SES, learn more in small schools than in large schools.
   b. High-SES students learn more in large schools, but low-SES students learn more in small schools.
   c. All students learn more in schools that are not too large nor too small, but the reduction in learning in very large schools is greater for *high*-SES than for *low*-SES students.
   d. All students learn more in schools that are not too large nor too small, but the reduction in learning in very large schools is greater for *low*-SES than for *high*-SES students.

28. Based on research, which of the following best describes the relationship between socioeconomic status, class size, and learning? (Small classes are defined as having about 15 students, and large classes are defined as having about 30 students.)

    a.   All students learn more in small classes, particularly in the lower grades and in inner-city schools.

    b.   Low-SES students learn more in small classes, but high-SES students learn more in large classes.

    c.   All students learn more in large classes since the amount of interaction among the students is likely to be greater in large classes.

    d.   Low-SES students learn more in small elementary school classes but less in small high school classes; high-SES students learn more in large classes at all levels.

29. According to research, which of the following statements best describes the relationship between students' attitudes about safety and order in their schools?

    a.   More than half of students responding to researchers' questions said that they preferred classrooms that weren't too strict and that occasional disruptions were actually "sort of fun."

    b.   Two thirds of students responding to researchers' questions said that the biggest problems in their classes were teachers who were too strict about student behavior.

    c.   Two thirds of students responding to researchers' questions said that other students disrupting classes was a problem in their schools.

    d.   Fewer than 10 percent of students responding to researchers' questions said that disruptions by other students in classes were a problem.

30. Which of the following statements best describes *personal teaching efficacy*?

    a.   A belief that the feelings and self-esteem of students is the most important goal for schools

    b.   A belief in the development of the student as a whole person, with emphasis on physical, intellectual, emotional, and social development

    c.   A belief that student motivation is the most important goal for schools and that students should be in charge of their own learning

    d.   A belief that teachers can promote learning in all students regardless of their background or ability

31. Which of the following characteristics do parents and other taxpayers view as most important for an effective school?

    a.   Effective instruction

    b.   High student test scores

    c.   Teachers with high personal teaching efficacy

    d.   School safety

32. Research indicates that two factors related to school organization have a particularly negative effect on cultural minorities. These two factors are

    a.   low teacher efficacy and class size.

    b.   class size and tracking.

    c.   low teacher efficacy and tracking.

    d.   ineffective instruction and large classes.

33. Tracking is common practice in comprehensive high schools. Of the following which statement most accurately describes the relationship between tracking and cultural minorities?

    a.   Tracking allows cultural minorities to achieve at levels consistent with their background and abilities.

    b.   A disproportionate number of cultural minorities tend to be placed in high-level tracks, where the instruction is too abstract for their background and abilities.

    c.   Tracking is effective for cultural minorities because it allows teachers to focus on the individual needs of students.

    d.   A disproportionate number of cultural minorities tend to be placed in low-level tracks, where instruction is often less effective than instruction in high-level tracks.

Items for Analysis and Critical Thinking

Leroy Williams works at Oceanside Middle School in a suburb of a medium-sized eastern city. His responsibilities include scheduling, collecting student records such as grades from teachers, keeping master records for the school, and maintaining communication with district-level administrators and parents.

Juanita Alvarez also works at Oceanside Middle School. Her duties at the school include scheduling and coordinating the statewide assessment tests that all the students are required to take and providing a variety of information about course offerings and future options for students.

34. Based on the way schools are typically organized, of the following Leroy is most likely to be
    a. a department head in the school (such as the head of the social studies department).
    b. the school principal.
    c. a vice principal in the school.
    d. a guidance counselor at the school.

35. Based on the way schools are typically organized, of the following Juanita is most likely to be
    a. the school principal.
    b. a vice principal at the school.
    c. an assistant principal at the school.
    d. a guidance counselor at the school.

36. You're a teacher at Oceanside Middle School, and Karen Adams, one of your students, comes to you complaining of a serious headache. Of the following which is your most acceptable course of action?
    a. Offer her one or two Advil tablets since you keep a bottle of them in your desk and Karen's problem seems to be limited to her headache.
    b. Send her to the school nurse since teachers are forbidden from administering any form of medication.
    c. Call one of the school assistant principals and ask his or her advice since a student may not be sent out of a classroom without an administrator's permission.
    d. Call Karen's mother, since any medical problem, including something as minor as a headache, must be immediately reported to a parent.

37. David Leech, one of your students, is consistently disrupting instruction in one of your classes. You've tried talking to him, giving him detention, and calling his parents. Nothing has worked, and you need help, feeling as though you're at your wits' end. Of the following who is the most appropriate person in the school to contact?
    a. The school principal since he or she is ultimately responsible for the school's operation
    b. One of the school assistant principals since student discipline is likely to be one of his or her duties
    c. Your grade-level chairperson or department head (such as the chair of the third grade in an elementary school or the head of the English department in a middle or high school)
    d. The school nurse since a chronically disruptive student is likely to have a medical problem

38. You want your students to identify subjects and verbs in sentences, so you plan to first teach the meaning of subjects, then the meaning of verbs, followed by having students identify them in sentences. Of the following your thinking in this case is best described as focusing on
    a. instructional design.
    b. developmental differences in students.
    c. school organization.
    d. curriculum organization.

39. Kelly, a fourth grader, is cooperative and able to consider other students' perspectives in cooperative learning activities, whereas Joanne tends to be quite self-centered. These characteristics most likely reflect differences in which of the following?
    a. Academic development
    b. Cognitive development
    c. Social development
    d. Physical development

40. Ann Peterson is teaching the same group of students in the fourth grade this year that she had in the third grade last year. This process is commonly described as
   a. looping.
   b. cooperative learning.
   c. peer tutoring.
   d. nurturing.

Use the following information for Items 41 and 42:

Jana, a first-grade teacher; Juan, a third-grade teacher; Suzanne, a fourth-grade teacher; and Vincent, a fifth-grade teacher want to use cooperative learning (where students are placed in groups and are expected to work collaboratively to meet a common goal) in their classrooms. All four are veterans, teach in the same school, and are viewed as highly skilled professionals.

41. If each teacher's students fit patterns typical for their ages, the teacher for whom implementing cooperative learning is likely to be most challenging is
   a. Jana.
   b. Juan.
   c. Suzanne.
   d. Vincent.

42. If each teacher's students fit patterns typical for their ages, the teacher for whom implementing cooperative learning is likely to be *least* challenging is
   a. Jana.
   b. Juan.
   c. Suzanne.
   d. Vincent.

43. Four teachers—Karen, a math teacher; Tony, who teaches science; Judy, an English teacher; and Alicia, who teaches social studies—have a common planning period. Today they're discussing ways of coordinating topics across the four content areas. Based on this information it's most likely that these teachers teach in a(n)
   a. elementary school.
   b. middle school.
   c. junior high.
   d. high school.

Use the following information in answering Items 44–47:

Gilchrist Middle School is strongly committed to academics. Clubs, sports, and other extracurricular activities are important in the school, but classes are never canceled for extracurricular activities.

   Most of the teachers at Gilchrist believe that they can promote learning for all students regardless of their backgrounds, and the teachers take personal responsibility for ensuring that learning takes place. The principal of the school has involved the teachers in a great deal of professional development designed to help them develop their questioning skills.

   Most of the teachers at Gilchrist give students a quiz at least once a week. The teachers then go over the quizzes with the students and carefully discuss frequently missed questions.

   Ridgeview Middle School is across town from Gilchrist and has a student population of similar SES. Its orientation is different from Gilchrist's. It believes that too much emphasis on academics for middle school children can impair their overall development. Consistent with this belief, they strongly emphasize the social aspects of development, involving students in discussion groups that examine a wide range of topics. The teachers at Ridgeview endorse the emphasis, noting, "In some cases, because of the background of the kids, we can't do a whole lot about their academics, but we can help develop self-esteem."

   Ridgeview's teachers emphasize orderly classrooms where the students carefully listen while the teachers clearly explain the topics they're teaching. "Many of these kids lack the background needed to answer questions," they note, "so we try to provide the background with clear explanations."

The teachers at Ridgeview de-emphasize testing because of the potential damage it can have on the way students feel about themselves.

44. Based on research examining the effectiveness of schools which of the following statements is most valid?
    a. Gilchrist is a more effective school than Ridgeview because of its academic orientation, but it is less effective because of its emphasis on testing.
    b. Ridgeview is a more effective school overall because it focuses on students' total development.
    c. Gilchrist is a more effective school overall because of its academic focus, attitude of the teachers, and emphasis on assessment.
    d. Ridgeview is a more effective school overall because of its emphasis on social development and self-esteem, and its de-emphasis on testing.

45. Consider the collective efficacy of the two schools. Based on effective schools research which of the following statements is most accurate?
    a. The collective efficacy of Gilchrist is higher than that of Ridgeview because the teachers believe they can get all students to learn.
    b. The collective efficacy of Ridgeview is higher than that of Gilchrist because the teachers at Ridgeview emphasize student self-esteem.
    c. The collective efficacy of Gilchrist is higher than that of Ridgeview because Gilchrist's principal has provided professional development opportunities for the teachers.
    d. The collective efficacy of Ridgeview is higher than that of Gilchrist because Gilchrist's teachers place too much emphasis on testing.

46. Consider the quality of instruction at the two schools. Based on effective schools research which of the following statements is most accurate?
    a. The instruction at Gilchrist is more effective than the instruction at Ridgeview because the Gilchrist teachers are higher in personal teaching efficacy.
    b. The instruction at Ridgeview is more effective than the instruction at Gilchrist because the Ridgeview teachers emphasize being able to provide clear explanations to students.
    c. The instruction at Ridgeview is more effective than the instruction at Gilchrist because the teachers more strongly emphasize student self-esteem at Ridgeview.
    d. The instruction at Gilchrist is more effective than the instruction at Ridgeview because the teachers at Gilchrist use more questioning than do the teachers at Ridgeview.

47. Based on research examining the collective efficacy of schools, which of the following statements is most accurate?
    a. High-SES students will achieve more than low-SES students at both schools, but the achievement gap between high- and low-SES students will be greater at Gilchrist than at Ridgeview.
    b. High-SES students will achieve more than low-SES students at both schools, but the achievement gap between high- and low-SES students will be greater at Ridgeview than at Gilchrist.
    c. High- and low-SES students will achieve at approximately the same levels at Ridgeview, but high-SES students will achieve more than low-SES students at Gilchrist.
    d. High- and low-SES students will achieve at approximately the same levels at Gilchrist, but high-SES students will achieve more than low-SES students at Ridgeview.

Extended-Response Items

48. Consider the concept *social institution*. Now take one of two positions: (a) The family is a social institution, or (b) the family is not a social institution. Defend your position based on your understanding of social institutions. (4 points)

49. Schools tend to be organized into elementary schools that are kindergarten (or pre-K) through grades 5 or 6; middle or junior high schools, which include some combination of grades 6–9; and high schools, which are grades 9 or 10 through 12. At least two reasons exist for this system of organization. Identify the reasons, and explain your answers. (4 points)

50. Comprehensive high schools are commonly criticized for at least two reasons. Identify the reasons, and explain your answers. (4 points)

51. Describe the concept *personal teaching efficacy*. Explain how it relates to the concept *high-collective-efficacy* school. Explain why both concepts are important. (6 points)

52. Explain how high- and low-collective-efficacy schools differ in both general student achievement and achievement differences between high- and low-SES students. (4 points)

53. Identify six characteristics of an effective school, and explain each characteristic. (12 points)

CHAPTER EIGHT

GOVERNANCE AND FINANCE: REGULATING AND FUNDING SCHOOLS

Knowledge-Level Items

1. With respect to education, which of the following best describes the significance of the Tenth Amendment to the Constitution?
   a. It established the principle of separation of church and state.
   b. It set land aside for the purpose of funding public education in the United States.
   c. It assigned legal responsibility for the education of citizens to the 50 states.
   d. It mandated that all teachers must be licensed in order to teach students in public school classrooms.

2. Which of the following statements best describes the similarities and differences in states' approaches to governing education?
   a. Most states have organizational structures that are unique to the geographical, economic, and political characteristics of the states.
   b. States in similar parts of the country—such as the Northeast, the Midwest, and the deep South—have similar organizational structures that differ significantly from the organizational structures in other parts of the country.
   c. States with large urban populations, such as New York and California, have similar organizational structures that differ significantly from the organizational structures of rural states, such as Wyoming and South Dakota.
   d. In spite of differences in geography, economy, and politics, each of the 50 states has a surprisingly similar organizational structure.

3. Approximately what percentage of a school district's education budget is supplied by states?
   a. 15 percent
   b. 45 percent
   c. 65 percent
   d. 85 percent

4. State boards of education regulate and advise schools by doing which of the following?
   (1) Hiring and releasing teachers
   (2) Establishing the length of the school year
   (3) Issuing and revoking teaching licenses
   (4) Publishing standards for accrediting schools
   (5) Implementing a system for gathering educational data (such as standardized tests.)

   a. 1, 2, 3, 4, 5
   b. 2, 3, 4, 5
   c. 1, 2, 3, 4
   d. 1, 2, 4, 5

5. Which of the following best describes the relationship between state *boards* of education and state *offices* of education?
   a. State boards make policies, and state offices implement policies for individual states.
   b. Both state boards and state offices make policies, which are then implemented by school districts in individual states.
   c. State boards provide the philosophical foundations for policies, which are then made by state offices for individual states.
   d. State boards make policies, which are implemented by individual districts and are evaluated by state offices for individual states.

6. Which of the following best describes the staffing of state boards of education and state offices of education?
   a. State boards are staffed by professional educators, whereas state offices are staffed by lay people (people who are not trained as professional educators).
   b. Both state boards and state offices are staffed by professional educators.
   c. Both state boards and state offices are staffed by lay people, who hire professional educators as consultants.
   d. State boards are staffed by lay people, whereas state offices are staffed by professional educators.

7. As a new teacher to which of the following will you apply for an initial teaching license?
   a. The state board of education for your state
   b. The state office of education for your state
   c. The commissioner of education for your state
   d. The local district in which you hope to teach

8. A geographical area given the legal responsibility for education within its borders is best described as a
   a. school system.
   b. school testing region.
   c. school district.
   d. state board of education.

9. Which of the following is given the responsibility for determining the curriculum that will be taught at an individual school?
   a. The state office of education for the state
   b. The local school district in which the curriculum is taught
   c. The local school in which the curriculum is taught
   d. The individual teacher within the school in which the curriculum is taught

10. Which of the following exists in every school district?
   (1) A district superintendent
   (2) A district school board
   (3) A district central staff
   (4) A district curriculum council
   (5) A district school-community relations council

   a. 1, 2, 3, 4, 5
   b. 1, 2, 3, 4
   c. 1, 2, 3, 5
   d. 1, 2, 3

11. Of the following what is the best description of a local school board?
   a. Groups of elected lay citizens responsible for setting school district policy
   b. Groups of trained education professionals appointed by state committees
   c. Groups of elected citizens who have earned at least bachelor's degrees at accredited colleges or universities
   d. Groups of district teachers, elected by their individual schools, who advise the superintendent on matters of district policy

12. Which of the following is *not* a function of local school boards?
   a. Implementing curriculum guidelines specified at state levels
   b. Specifying teaching techniques that increase student achievement
   c. Raising and disbursing money to schools within the district
   d. Hiring and firing individual teachers in schools

13. Which of the following is responsible for defining the curriculum and implementing general guidelines developed by states?
   a. State-level education boards
   b. Local school boards
   c. Individual schools (led by school principals)
   d. Individual teachers

14. Which of the following best describes the typical composition of local school boards?
   a. Male, cultural minority, lower SES, older (over 40)
   b. Female, white, older, wealthy
   c. Male, white, young, lower SES
   d. Male, white, older, wealthy

15. Which of the following is a school district's head administrative officer?
   a. The state superintendent of education
   b. The district superintendent
   c. The chairperson of the local school board
   d. A school principal elected by all the teachers in the district

16. Which of the following is responsible for overseeing the implementation of policies in a school district's schools?
   a. A staff member from the state's office of education
   b. The local school board
   c. The district's superintendent and his or her staff
   d. The principals of each school in a district

17. The person(s) most responsible for establishing and maintaining high expectations for teachers and students is(are)
   a. the superintendent for the local school district.
   b. the local school board for the district.
   c. the principal of the individual school.
   d. the teachers themselves in the individual school.

18. With respect to promoting student learning, which of the following is(are) often considered to be the most important person(s) in a school district's administrative structure?
   a. The members of the local school board
   b. The district superintendent
   c. The district superintendent's staff (such as a math or science curriculum specialist for the local district)
   d. The principal of each local school

19. Of the following, according to a Gallup poll examining public opinion, which is the biggest problem facing local schools?
   a. Ineffectively prepared teachers
   b. Inadequate school leadership (such as underqualified school principals)
   c. Inadequate district leadership (such as lack of effective leadership from the district superintendent)
   d. Lack of financial support and funding for the schools

20. Of the following which best describes the respective proportion of funding that schools receive from local, state, and federal sources?
   a. Local and state shares are about equal, and the federal share is much smaller.
   b. State and federal shares are about equal, and local shares are much smaller.
   c. Local sources provide about three fourths of all funding, with the remaining fourth being about evenly split between state and federal sources.
   d. Each of the three sources provides about the same proportion of the funding for local districts.

21. The majority (about three fourths) of funding for schools at the local level comes from which of the following?
   a.   Traffic fines
   b.   Federal and state grants
   c.   Fees for building permits
   d.   Property taxes

22. For most states in the United States the largest source of revenue is which of the following?
   a.   Sales taxes
   b.   State income taxes
   c.   Property taxes
   d.   Sin taxes (such as taxes on cigarettes and alcohol)

23. Of the following which best approximates the percentage of educational funding that comes from the federal government?
   a.   Slightly more than 5 percent
   b.   About 15 percent
   c.   About 25 percent
   d.   About 50 percent

24. Funding for schools—at the local, state, and federal level—is controversial. Which of the following best describes the controversies involved in educational funding?
   a.   Local funding is most controversial because property owners who don't have children in the local schools feel they should not have to pay taxes to fund schools.
   b.   Local funding is most controversial because large differences exist in districts' tax bases.
   c.   State funding is most controversial because money derived from lotteries reduces money that education receives from other sources.
   d.   Federal funding is most controversial because proponents believe education is essential for the progress of the country, whereas critics warn of too much federal control of education.

25. Which of the following best describes the source of funding for programs such as Title I, Head Start, and the Bilingual Education Act of 1972?
   a.   The programs are funded by federal categorical grants and block grants.
   b.   The programs are funded by state categorical grants and block grants.
   c.   The programs are funded by federal categorical grants (but not block grants).
   d.   The programs are funded by federal block grants (but not categorical grants).

26. Based on research examining educational expenditures and educational quality, which of the following is the most accurate statement?
   a.   Little relationship exists between the amount of money spent on education per pupil and the amount students learn.
   b.   Increased educational funding improves school physical facilities (such as school buildings), but little evidence of improved learning exists.
   c.   Increased educational funding results in better qualified teachers and smaller class sizes, which causes increased learning.
   d.   Increased educational funding increases the size of administrative staffs but does little to improve working conditions for teachers.

27. Of the following which best approximates the percentage of the money allocated to education that is actually spent on instruction?
   a.   10 percent
   b.   25 percent
   c.   60 percent
   d.   85 percent

28. Of the following which best describes the comparison between the amount of education money that is spent on administration and maintenance of schools compared to administration and maintenance of physical plants in industry?

    a.   Education spends a much higher percentage of its total budget (about 50% more) on administration and the maintenance of schools than does industry for its administration and maintenance of physical plants.

    b.   Education spends a slightly higher percentage of its total budget (about 5% more) on administration and the maintenance of schools than does industry for its administration and maintenance of physical plants.

    c.   Education and industry spend comparable percentages of their total budgets on administration and the maintenance of schools and physical plants.

    d.   Education spends a significantly lower percentage of its total budget (about 20% less) on administration and the maintenance of schools than does industry for its administration and maintenance of physical plants.

29. Of the following which is the closest approximate percentage of local school districts' education budgets that is supplied by their states (such as a local district in Missouri receiving funds from the state of Missouri)?

    a.   10 percent
    b.   25 percent
    c.   45 percent
    d.   75 percent

30. Of the following which is the most accurate estimate of yearly per-pupil spending in the United States?

    a. $2,000
    b. $6,000
    c. $10,000
    d. $15,000

31. Of the following which is the best approximation of the range of yearly per-pupil spending in the United States?

    a. $2,000 to $5,000
    b. $5,000 to $8,000
    c. $5,000 to $11,000
    d. $10,000 to $15,000

32. Which of the following best describes site-based decision making?

    a.   A movement toward placing more responsibility for governance of schools in the hands of teachers and parents

    b.   A movement toward equalizing funding by moving funds from rich districts to school-district sites that are underfunded

    c.   A movement toward training teachers on site instead of having them trained at colleges or universities

    d.   A movement toward requiring that local school board members be trained educators (instead of lay people)

33. The concept of school choice most commonly brings to mind which of the following?

  (1) Charter schools
  (2) School vouchers
  (3) Home schooling
  (4) Alternative schools

    a.   1, 2, 3, 4
    b.   1, 2, 3
    c.   1, 3, 4
    d.   1, 2

34. Which of the following best describes a charter school?
   a. A private school that is partially funded by school vouchers
   b. A religious school that receives public funding (such as money that comes from personal property taxes) to help educate students with exceptionalities
   c. A school that is publically funded (such as with money from property taxes) but is governed independent of the structure of a local school district
   d. A school that is publically funded but is governed by a local advisory council appointed by the local school board of the district in which the school exists

35. According to research which is the most accurate assessment of for-profit charter schools (designed to make money for the people managing the school)?
   a. The educational experiences they provide for students are generally superior to the experiences students have in public schools.
   b. The educational experiences they provide for students are generally about equivalent to the experiences students have in public schools.
   c. The educational experiences they provide for students are generally superior to the experiences students have in public schools and about equivalent to the experiences not-for-profit charter schools provide.
   d. The educational experiences they provide for students are generally inferior to the experiences students have in public schools.

36. Which of the following best describes vouchers?
   a. Written applications that people who want to open charter schools submit to local school boards
   b. Financial support that parents can use to purchase educational services at schools other than the ones their children are attending
   c. Written descriptions of the governance structure for schools committed to site-based decision making
   d. Federal funding for private schools to support the education of students with learning disabilities

37. Which of the following best describes state tax-credit plans?
   a. Tax credits parents receive for money they've spent on private school tuition
   b. Tax credits local school districts receive for implementing charter schools
   c. Tax credits districts with low property tax bases receive to make funding between rich and poor districts more equitable
   d. Tax credits individual schools receive for implementing site-based decision-making plans

38. "The ultimate form of school choice" is best described as which of the following?
   a. Charter schools
   b. Vouchers
   c. Home schooling
   d. State tuition tax credits

Items for Analysis and Critical Thinking

39. You're a teacher serving on a curriculum committee that is searching for a new textbook series for math. Which of the following statements best describes the parameters (if any) within which you must operate?
   a. There are no parameters within which you must operate. Your committee can select the series you believe is highest in quality.
   b. You must select a textbook series that is on a state-approved list.
   c. You are encouraged to select a textbook series that is on a state-approved list, but you may select a series that isn't on the list if your district approves your selection.
   d. You must select a series that is on both a state-approved list and a district-approved list.

40. You have just secured your first teaching job. If your district is consistent with historical trends in the creation of school districts, which of the following is most likely?
- a. You are likely to teach in a smaller district than in the past since the trend is toward the creation of smaller school districts that are more personalized for both teachers and students.
- b. If you're teaching in a rural area, you're likely to be teaching in a larger district than in the past but if you're teaching in a large city, you're likely to teach in a smaller district than in the past since the trend is toward larger school districts in rural areas (such as sparsely populated areas of Wyoming, Montana, and Nevada) but toward smaller school districts in large cities (such as New York and Chicago).
- c. You're likely to teach in a larger district than in the past since the trend is toward fewer and larger school districts, in general, across the country.
- d. If your job is in the South or the West, you're likely to be teaching in a larger district than in the past but if you're teaching in the Midwest or the Northeast, you're likely to be teaching in a smaller district than in the past since the population of the United States is moving south and west.

41. You've just been hired for your first teaching position. Which of the following best describes the composition and selection of members of the local school board for the school district in which you're teaching?
- a. Local school boards are composed of lay people (people who are not trained as professional educators) appointed by superintendents of the districts in which they serve.
- b. Local school boards are composed of professional educators selected by the city governments in which they serve.
- c. Local school boards are composed of professional educators who are elected by the citizens of the districts in which they serve.
- d. Local school boards are composed of lay people who are elected by the citizens of the districts in which they serve.

42. You're working in your first teaching job, and the issue comes up of a student in one of your classes missing school to participate in a foreign exchange program. Which of the following is most responsible for establishing the general policies for student attendance in this case?
- a. The state office of education for your state
- b. The local school board for your district
- c. The school in which you teach
- d. You

43. You're a high school teacher, and the students in your school are allowed to participate in sports only if they maintain a *C* average for all their courses. Of the following the group most responsible for setting this policy is
- a. the local school board for the district in which you teach.
- b. the administration for your school (the principal and vice principal or assistant principals).
- c. the administration for your school with input from the teachers in the school.
- d. the teachers in your school (working through the school's committee structure).

44. You're applying for a job. Of the following which will be most influential in determining whether or not you get the job?
- a. The local school board for the district in which you want to teach
- b. The district superintendent for the district in which you want to teach
- c. The school principal for the school in which you want to teach
- d. A committee composed of teachers in the school (a search committee) in which you want to teach

45. You've taken a job in a school district, and you've agreed to teach in an inner-city school. When you enter the school for the first time, you're uneasy, seeing that the school building is somewhat run down, the school is not air conditioned, and textbooks in some of the curriculum areas are outdated. You're surprised because you recently visited a school in a different district only a few miles away, and the school was very modern and well equipped. Which of the following is the most likely reason for the difference in the two schools?
   a. The administration of the first school is less effective than the administration of the second school.
   b. The goals for the local school board in the first district aren't as clear as are the goals for the local school board in the second district.
   c. The first school doesn't have a mission that is as clear and focused as is the mission for the second school.
   d. The property taxes in the first district are lower than the property taxes in the second district.

46. You've taken a job in a school that is committed to site-based decision making. Of the following which is most likely to happen in your school (compared to a school not committed to site-based decision making)?
   a. Expectations for student achievement are likely to be higher at your school than they are at a school not committed to site-based decision making.
   b. Your school is likely to have more administrators than a school not committed to site-based decision making.
   c. Your school is likely to have a wider array of extracurricular activities for students than a school not committed to site-based decision making.
   d. You're likely to spend considerably more time in committee work than you would at a school not committed to site-based decision making.

Extended-Response Items

47. Identify and explain one advantage and one disadvantage of both a small and a large school district. (8 points)

48. Describe five functions of local school boards, and provide an example that illustrates each. (10 points)

49. Describe two important disparities between the composition of school boards and the people they serve. Explain why these disparities are important. (4 points)

50. Describe and explain two important disadvantages in using property taxes as the basis for funding schools in local districts. (4 points)

51. Describe and explain the most important disadvantage of sales taxes as sources of revenue for states. (2 points)

52. Describe the difference between federal block grants and federal categorical grants. Which type has most strongly influenced education at the local level? Explain your answer to the question. (5 points)

53. Describe the controversy involved in the issue of school choice. Include and explain both sides of the argument. (4 points)

CHAPTER NINE

SCHOOL LAW: ETHICAL AND LEGAL INFLUENCES ON TEACHING

Knowledge-Level Items

1. Of the following what is the best definition of a professional?
   a. A person able to complete tasks according to well-defined criteria
   b. A person able to make decisions in ill-defined situations
   c. A person who cares about the well-being of young people
   d. A person who is able to effectively explain complex forms of knowledge

2. Of the following which best describes laws that regulate the rights and responsibilities of teachers?
   a. They are purposely written in general terms so they can be applied to a variety of specific situations.
   b. They are written in very specific terms with the intent of avoiding misinterpretation.
   c. Laws describing teachers' responsibilities with respect to students' safety in school are written in very specific terms, whereas laws describing the required behavior of teachers in instructional situations are written in general terms.
   d. Laws regulating the professional preparation of teachers are very specific, and all other laws are described in general terms.

3. Of the following which best describes an important limitation of laws that regulate the rights and responsibilities of teachers?
   a. They are written so specifically that the huge volume of laws and regulations are virtually impossible to remember.
   b. The laws are written in response to problems in the past, so they don't necessarily apply to situations that exist today.
   c. The laws apply primarily to the protection of students, and few laws regulate the professional behavior of teachers.
   d. The laws apply primarily to the administration of schools within school districts, and they provide little guidance for individual teachers' decision making.

4. Which of the following is the best definition of *ethics*?
   a. Legal mandates that specify acceptable conduct for classroom teachers
   b. Constitutional amendments that provide standards for moral behavior
   c. School-district guidelines that outline teachers' responsibilities
   d. Principles used to decide whether acts are right or wrong

5. Which of the following statements best describes the relationship between teachers' legal responsibilities and their ethical responsibilities?
   a. Both their legal and their ethical responsibilities describe what teachers *must* do, as required by law, when they work with students.
   b. Their legal responsibilities describe the limitations for teachers (such as requiring that teachers avoid romantic relationships with students), whereas ethical responsibilities describe what teachers must do to protect students (such as intervening in an issue involving student safety).
   c. Legal responsibilities describe what teachers *must* do (such as protecting students' safety), whereas ethical responsibilities describe what teachers *should* do (such as objectively presenting both sides of a controversial issue).
   d. Legal responsibilities describe what teachers must do in working with administrators and colleagues, whereas ethical responsibilities describe what teachers must do in working with students.

6. Which of the following statements best describes codes of ethics in different professions?
   a. All professions have codes of ethics that are designed to guide practitioners and protect clients.
   b. Because helping young people learn is involved, education has a code of ethics, but other professions do not.
   c. Professions, such as medicine and education, that directly involve the health and education of people have codes of ethics, but professions that create products, such as architecture, do not.
   d. Professions that involve supervision from administrators, such as education, have codes of ethics, but professions with high levels of autonomy, such as medicine, do not.

7. A process designed to ensure that teachers are competent and morally fit to work with youth is best described as
   a. ethical endorsement.
   b. validation.
   c. accountability.
   d. licensure.

8. A legal agreement between a teacher and a local school board is best described as
   a. teacher licensure.
   b. a teaching contract.
   c. a code of ethics.
   d. a high-stakes test.

9. Which of the following is the best description of teacher tenure?
   a. Protection from dismissal without cause and without observing due process
   b. Promotion to the rank of tenured teacher after completing 3 years of experience and earning an advanced degree
   c. Protection from dismissal except in cases of overstaffing or reduced student enrollments
   d. Protection from dismissal except in cases of "riffing" (reduction in force)

10. For which of the following may a new teacher be legally dismissed?
    (1) Incompetence
    (2) Overstaffing
    (3) Controversial political views
    (4) Reduced student enrollments
    (5) Dishonesty in a job application

       a. 1, 2, 3, 4, 5
       b. 1, 2, 4, 5
       c. 1, 3, 5
       d. 1, 3, 4 5

11. For which of the following may a tenured teacher be legally dismissed?
    (1) Incompetence
    (2) Controversial political views
    (3) Immoral behavior
    (4) Unethical conduct
    (5) Insubordination

       a. 1, 2, 3, 4, 5
       b. 1, 3, 4, 5
       c. 1, 2, 3, 4
       d. 1, 3, 4

12. A tenured teacher in your school has been charged with gross incompetence, and the school is following due process procedures. This teacher's rights to due process are protected by
   a. local school policies.
   b. local district policies.
   c. state law.
   d. federal law.

13. Which of the following best describes the practice called reduction in force ("riffing")?
   a. The process of eliminating incompetent teachers before they're given tenure
   b. The process of eliminating nontenured teachers in the event of declining student numbers, program cancellations, or budget cuts
   c. The process of eliminating either tenured or nontenured teachers in the event of declining student numbers, program cancellations, or budget cuts
   d. The process of eliminating tenured teachers who have demonstrated incompetence for 3 consecutive years

14. Teachers' rights to choose content and teaching methods based on their professional judgment is best described as
   a. due process.
   b. tenure.
   c. freedom of speech.
   d. academic freedom.

15. Of the following which is the best description of academic freedom?
   a. Teachers' rights to choose both the content to be taught and the methods used to teach the content based on their professional judgment
   b. Teachers' rights to choose the methods to be used to deliver the curriculum but not the content of the curriculum itself
   c. Teachers' rights to make decisions about the ethical treatment of students based on the general guidelines of the National Education Association code of ethics
   d. Teachers' rights to have input into administrative decisions that ensure the smooth functioning of the school

16. Policies that specify limitations on the use of print, video, and software materials are best described as
   a. copyright laws.
   b. fair use guidelines.
   c. academic principles.
   d. academic freedom.

17. A principle requiring teachers to use the same judgment and care as parents in protecting children under their supervision is best identified as
   a. a code of ethics.
   b. academic freedom.
   c. unconditional positive regard.
   d. in loco parentis.

18. To prevent charges of negligence, for which of the following are teachers always responsible?
   (1) Making reasonable attempts to anticipate dangerous situations
   (2) Establishing procedures to prevent injuries
   (3) Warning students of possible dangerous situations
   (4) Providing proper supervision
   (5) Preventing student injury

   a.   1, 2, 3, 4, 5
   b.   1, 2, 3, 4
   c.   2, 3, 4, 5
   d.   1, 3, 4

19. Of the following which is the best description of notoriety?
   a.   A teacher being prosecuted for violating a copyright law
   b.   A teacher with AIDS failing to report his or her condition to school authorities
   c.   A teacher committing a felony
   d.   A teacher behaving in a way that becomes known and controversial

20. Of the following what is the most important factor in determining court decisions about teachers' private behavior?
   a.   Context: is the behavior consistent with the norms of behavior for the community in which the teacher works?
   b.   Notoriety: is the teacher's behavior well-known and controversial?
   c.   Leadership: does the school leadership condone or condemn the behavior?
   d.   Religion: does the teacher's behavior violate the prevailing religious beliefs for the community in which the teacher works?

21. Which of the following statements best describes the law with respect to teachers' private sexual lives?
   a.   The law is ambiguous with respect to teachers' private sexual lives; court decisions have historically varied.
   b.   Once under contract, teachers are legally prohibited from having sexual experiences outside marriage; teachers' past sexual experiences are not an issue.
   c.   The law is ambiguous with respect to teachers' private sexual lives except in relationships with students; a sexual relationship with a student will result in dismissal.
   d.   Teachers are legally restricted from having sexual relationships with students or colleagues, but the law does not address teachers' sexual lives outside the professional environment.

22. Which of the following best describes students' freedom of speech rights?
   a.   Students have the right of freedom of speech as guaranteed by the U.S. Constitution, and this right may not be violated by schools.
   b.   Students have the right of freedom of speech unless expression of this freedom interferes with learning or running the school.
   c.   Students have the right of freedom of speech if expression of that right is related to the school curriculum, but they do not have the right to freedom of speech outside the school curriculum.
   d.   Students have the right of freedom of speech about any issue that is expressed in the context of extracurricular activities (such as a speech club), but their freedom of speech rights are restricted to the curriculum in the regular classroom.

23. Which of the following best describes students' rights with respect to permissible search and seizure?
    a. The Fourth Amendment to the Constitution protects all citizens from unlawful search and seizure, so students' personal belongings may not be searched by school officials.
    b. Since school safety has become an issue, school officials are allowed to search students whenever they feel it is in the best interest of school safety.
    c. School officials may search students' personal belongings if they have reasonable suspicion (probable cause) that a problem exists.
    d. The Fourth Amendment to the Constitution does not apply to school settings, and students' personal belongings may be searched at any time.

24. Which of the following best describes the most common outcome in court cases involving students with AIDS?
    a. Students with AIDS are not allowed to attend public schools because of the health risks involved.
    b. Students with AIDS are not allowed to attend public schools because they're unable to complete the work typically required in the school curriculum.
    c. Students with AIDS are allowed to attend public schools without restriction.
    d. Students with AIDS are allowed to attend public schools with special safeguards to prevent blood spills.

25. Which of the following best describes affirmative action?
    a. Policies and procedures that define when religious beliefs may be affirmed in schools
    b. Policies that outline due process for both teachers and students when they're accused of unprofessional or illegal conduct
    c. Policies that affirm parents' rights to access their children's private records and prevent other people from the same access
    d. Policies and procedures designed to overcome past discrimination that has occurred on the basis of race, ethnicity, gender, or disability

26. A clause that prohibits the creation of a national religion in the United States is best described as
    a. the establishment clause of the First Amendment to the Constitution.
    b. the free exercise clause of the First Amendment to the Constitution.
    c. the freedom of religion clause of the Fourteenth Amendment to the Constitution.
    d. the separation of church and state clause of the Fourteenth Amendment to the Constitution.

27. A clause that prohibits the government from interfering with individuals' rights to hold and practice the religion of their choice is best described as
    a. the establishment clause of the First Amendment to the Constitution.
    b. the free exercise clause of the First Amendment to the Constitution.
    c. the freedom of religion clause of the First Amendment to the Constitution.
    d. the separation of church and state clause of the First Amendment to the Constitution.

28. Which of the following is the best description of the law commonly known as the Buckley Amendment?
    a. A legal act that prevents the teaching in public schools of biblical descriptions of the creation of humanity
    b. A legal act that prevents teachers from being terminated without access to due process
    c. A legal act that makes school records more open and accessible to parents
    d. A legal act that prevents students from being expelled without due process

Items for Analysis and Critical Thinking

29. As a new teacher you realize that your legal rights and responsibilities and codes of ethics are limited because they provide only general guidelines for your professional practice. Of the following what is the most effective and practical process you can use to accommodate the general nature of laws and ethics?
   a. Know as many of the laws that apply to education as possible, and keep your code of ethics handy as a reference.
   b. In cases involving decision making, contact a supervisor, such as a grade-level chairperson, department head, or assistant principal.
   c. Develop a well-defined personal philosophy that will guide your specific decisions in your day-to-day work as a professional.
   d. Create a relationship with another teacher who can be your confidant and mentor to help you with your day-to-day decisions.

30. Which of the following best illustrates legal influence on you as a teacher that is generated by the federal government?
   a. You will be required to have a teaching license before you're allowed to accept a job as a teacher.
   b. You will be a candidate for tenure, most commonly after 3 years of successful teaching experience.
   c. You will be required to use a textbook from a state-adopted list.
   d. You will have cultural minorities in your classes as a result of the Civil Rights Act of 1964.

31. Suppose you've taken a job as a third-grade teacher. Which of the following best illustrates a legal influence on you that comes from your state?
   a. You are likely to have some students pulled out of your class because they are receiving Title I support.
   b. You are virtually certain to have some students with exceptionalities in your class because of the Individuals with Disabilities Education Act, which mandates that learners with exceptionalities be taught in as normal an education setting as possible.
   c. You will be required to have a teaching license before you are allowed to take the job in your school.
   d. You will have been hired as a result of a recruiting process that most likely includes an interview with your school principal.

32. As a beginning teacher you're likely to be asked to pass a competency test that measures basic skills, such as reading, writing, and math; your background in a content area, such as biology or history; and an understanding of learning and teaching. With respect to the legality of these tests, which of the following is the most accurate response?
   a. Although they are generally required for employment, you are not legally bound to take the tests in order to apply for employment.
   b. You will be legally bound to take the tests if you want to become eligible for a teaching license.
   c. Although you're not legally bound to take the tests, your chances for employment are reduced if the test results are not on your record.
   d. You are legally bound to take the tests if you don't have a degree in a specific content area, such as math; but if you have a degree, you're not legally bound to take the tests.

33. You have signed a contract to teach in a local school district, and later you decide that you want to take another job in a different state. Which of the following best describes your legal obligations?
   a. Although you're ethically bound by a teaching contract, you are not legally bound, and you can legally take the job in the other state.
   b. You are neither legally nor ethically bound by the contract since you want to move out of the state.
   c. You are legally bound by the contract, and in many states you could lose your license for breaking the contract.
   d. You are legally bound by the contract, and you could be subject to some forfeiture of your first-year salary if you take the job in the other state.

34. Which of the following best describes your legal obligations to perform nonteaching duties (such as serving as a sponsor for a debate club or a coach of an athletic team) as part of your teaching job?
   a. You have no legal obligations to perform nonteaching duties as part of your job.
   b. You are legally obligated to perform any nonteaching duties specified by your local school district's policies.
   c. You are legally obligated to perform nonteaching duties specified by your state, but your district cannot impose additional nonteaching duties.
   d. You are legally obligated to perform nonteaching duties specified by your local district's policies if the duties are connected to your teaching assignment (such as a science teacher being required to be a science club sponsor).

35. A first-year teacher in your school is not being offered a contract for her second year because the school enrollments have gone down and the teaching staff is being reduced. Which of the following best describes the teacher's legal rights?
   a. The school has to follow a due process procedure just as it would in the case of a tenured teacher being dismissed for incompetence.
   b. The school has to follow a due process procedure just as it would in the case of a nontenured teacher being dismissed for incompetence.
   c. In some states a hearing will be required, but in most states the teacher can be dismissed without a hearing.
   d. The teacher cannot be dismissed after the first year for any reason other than immoral behavior or committing a felony; once the teacher has signed a legal contract, a district is legally obligated to give a second year of employment.

36. A fifth-grade teacher, in an effort to motivate his students, allows them to go out and play on the playground for designated periods of time as a reward for turning in their homework on time. Students who don't turn in their homework on time are required to serve detention after school. The principal warns the teacher three times that this practice is unacceptable, but the teacher protests each time that the students' motivation has increased significantly as a result of this practice. The teacher is dismissed but then sues, arguing that his academic freedom has been violated. If this case is consistent with other cases involving academic freedom and freedom of speech, which of the following is the most likely outcome?
   a. The district's dismissal will be overturned in court since the students' motivation has increased.
   b. The district's dismissal will be overturned in court since playing on the playground is part of children's typical school activities.
   c. The district's dismissal will be upheld in court since the teacher used unconventional methods and was warned three times.
   d. The district's dismissal will be overturned in court because the teacher used both rewards (letting the students play) and punishers (keeping students after school) as part of his methods.

37. You're a high-school health teacher, and you're considering sexual abuse as a topic in your class. You want the students to understand the signs of sexual abuse as well as some of the emotions that can lead to sexual abuse. "I want to prevent sexual abuse if possible," you reason, "and the only way this will happen is through understanding." A number of parents complain, arguing that the topic is too controversial and it shouldn't be a part of the school curriculum. You defend your decision, citing academic freedom as a rationale. With respect to your academic freedom, which of the following is the most valid conclusion?
   a. Your right to teach the topic will likely be overturned since a number of parents have complained.
   b. Your right to teach the topic will likely be overturned because sexual abuse isn't part of the mainstream health curriculum.
   c. Your right to teach the topic will likely be upheld since you have cited academic freedom as a rationale.
   d. Your right to teach the topic will likely be upheld since you have a clear educational goal and rationale for wanting to teach the topic.

38. You want to tape a television program for use in your classroom. Which of the following statements best describes the copyright restriction in this case?
   a.   You may copy and show the program as many times as you want since television programs are not subject to copyright laws.
   b.   You may copy the program if given written permission by the network or independent station that airs the program.
   c.   You may copy the program and show it twice, but it must be erased within 45 days.
   d.   You may not legally copy any television program (even though many people do).

39. You're walking across the courtyard at your school and see two large boys pushing a smaller boy back and forth between them. None of the boys are in any of your classes. While the smaller boy doesn't seem to be hurt, he is shouting at the other boys to stop. Which of the following best describes your responsibility in this case?
   a.   You have no legal or ethical responsibility in this case since the boys are not in your classes.
   b.   You have no legal or ethical responsibility in this case since the incident is occurring outside your classroom.
   c.   You have no legal responsibility since the boys are not in your classes and the incident is occurring outside your classroom, but you have an ethical responsibility to protect the smaller boy's feelings.
   d.   You are legally required to intervene, and failing to do so is grounds for a lawsuit charging negligence.

40. You notice that Sanchia, one of your third graders, frequently comes to school disheveled and with bruises on her arms. When you ask her what caused the bruises, she says that she got them roughhousing with her older brothers. Suspecting child abuse, you report what you've seen to school authorities. After an investigation, it turns out that Sanchia has told the truth, and the bruises were indeed the result of roughhousing. Furious over the allegation of child abuse, Sanchia's mother, a single parent, files a lawsuit against you and the school. Of the following which is the most accurate assessment of your situation?
   a.   You are not protected from liability since you mistakenly alleged that the parents abused Sanchia.
   b.   You are not protected from liability since the only evidence of child abuse was Sanchia's disheveled appearance and bruises on her arms.
   c.   Because of the seriousness of child abuse, teachers are protected from liability in all allegations of child abuse, so you are protected from liability.
   d.   You are protected from liability since you honestly reported the allegation based on her disheveled appearance and bruises.

41. As a first-year teacher you went to a weekend party, had a bit too much to drink, and were picked up for and convicted of driving under the influence. With respect to your teaching job, of the following which is the most valid conclusion?
   a.   The incident has no professional implications for you as a teacher since it occurred outside normal working hours.
   b.   The incident has no legal implications for you as a teacher, but you may be reprimanded for a violation of professional ethics.
   c.   A description of the incident will be placed in your permanent record, and a second similar incident will result in a letter of reprimand.
   d.   The incident could result in dismissal since teachers are legally and ethically responsible for being role models for students.

42. A teacher in your school has been diagnosed with AIDS. If the issue is resolved in a way that is consistent with legal precedent, which of the following is the most likely legal decision?
   a.   The teacher will be dismissed since AIDS-infected teachers are a health risk to young people.
   b.   The teacher will be dismissed since AIDS-infected teachers are viewed as negative role models for students.
   c.   The teacher will be dismissed since AIDS-infected teachers don't have the energy to do their jobs effectively.
   d.   The teacher will be retained since the teacher's rights to employment outweigh the minor risk of infecting students.

43. A group of parents on your school advisory council believe that a prayer should be offered before school activities, such as assemblies, believing that expressions of religious belief promote a positive emotional climate in the school. If the issue is settled in a way that is consistent with legal precedent, which of the following is the most likely conclusion?

    a.   Prayer will be allowed if the prayer is said by a school administrator.

    b.   Prayer will be allowed if it is generic (not associated with a specific religion).

    c.   Prayer will be allowed if it is initiated by a student and doesn't interfere with other students or the functioning of the school.

    d.   Prayer will not be allowed under any circumstances.

44. A student in one of your classes asks you if she and some her friends can use your classroom for Christian bible study before school. You're not sure if this is a violation of the principle of separation of church and state. If this question was to become a legal issue and if a ruling was consistent with legal precedent, which of the following is the most valid conclusion?

    a.   The study group will not be allowed to meet on the school campus since it is associated with a particular religious organization.

    b.   The study group will be allowed to meet since schools must allow religious groups to use school facilities on the same basis as other extracurricular organizations.

    c.   The study group will not be allowed to meet because it establishes the possibility of undesirable groups, such as the Aryan Nation (a neo-Nazi organization), making a similar request.

    d.   The study group will not be allowed to meet since religious symbols (such as the bible) are not allowed in schools.

45. You're a high school teacher, and one of your colleagues has her senior English students reading Shakespeare's *Macbeth*. A parent group, arguing that the students are being exposed to witchcraft, sues the school, attempting to eliminate study of the play. Your colleague protests that the study of classic literature is an essential part of the curriculum. If a ruling in this case is consistent with legal precedent, which of the following is the most valid conclusion?

    a.   The courts will rule in favor of the school since studying the play has a clear purpose.

    b.   The courts will rule in favor of the parents since the play will be interpreted as advocating a particular religious belief.

    c.   The courts will rule in favor of the school since making curricular decisions is within the school's rights.

    d.   The courts will rule in favor of the parents since schools must be responsive to parental concerns.

46. You're a first-year teacher, you're very busy, and you've fallen behind on scoring your students' papers. To save some time, you decide to have the students exchange papers and score each other's tests (even though you don't do this as part of your typical routine). A parent protests, arguing that this procedure is unlawful because it discloses confidential information (child's test score) without consent. If the decision in this case is consistent with legal precedent, which of the following is the most likely conclusion?

    a.   A court decision would rule in favor of the parent, based on one of the provisions of the Buckley Amendment.

    b.   A court decision would rule in favor of the parent, based on the ethical principle of avoiding unnecessary embarrassment of a student.

    c.   A court decision would rule against the parent because this isn't part of your typical routine.

    d.   A court decision would rule against the parent because test scores on teacher-prepared tests aren't part of a child's permanent record.

Extended-Response Items

47. Describe two limitations of laws that regulate the rights and responsibilities of teachers. Illustrate each with a specific example. (4 points)

48. Describe an important limitation of codes of ethics for teachers, such as the National Education Association's code of ethics. Illustrate the limitation with a specific example. (2 points)

49. Describe five important features of a teacher's due process rights in the case of charges being filed for incompetence, immoral behavior, insubordination, or unprofessional conduct. (5 points)

50. Describe the copyright laws that regulate what materials you may reproduce. Include in your response a description of fair-use guidelines and the regulations for copying consumable materials (such as workbooks). (6 points)

51. Describe and explain the difference between in loco parentis and negligence. (4 points)

52. Describe the general guideline that exists with respect to teaching religious topics in schools. (3 points)

53. Describe parents' rights of access to their children's academic records as mandated by the Family Educational Rights and Privacy Act (FERPA) (the Buckley Amendment). Also, explain why the issue of academic records is so important. (5 points)

54. In states where it is legal, describe the conditions under which corporal punishment can be administered. Identify one important reason that corporal punishment is strongly discouraged by behavioral psychologists. (4 points)

55. Describe students' due process rights in cases of disciplinary action. How do these rights compare to teachers' in cases involving possible dismissal? (3 points)

CHAPTER TEN

THE SCHOOL CURRICULUM

Knowledge-Level Items

1. Which of the following statements best describes *curriculum*?
    a. Learning goals and the reasons the goals have been selected
    b. Learning goals and the way the goals will be accomplished
    c. Learning goals, the reasons for having the goals, and the way the goals will be accomplished
    d. Learning goals based on students' emotional needs

2. Which of the following best describes *instruction*?
    a. Learning goals and the reasons the goals have been selected
    b. The ways teachers help students reach learning goals
    c. Learning goals and a diagnosis of students' needs
    d. Learning goals and the philosophy on which the goals are based

3. Which of the following best describes the explicit curriculum?
    a. What students learn as communicated through the kinds of routines teachers establish
    b. What students learn in clubs and organizations (such as a science club)
    c. What students learn through the ways teachers interact with them
    d. What students learn that is found in their textbooks

4. Of the following which is the most accurate description of curriculum in elementary schools?
    a. Strong emphasis on science and math and relatively little emphasis on reading and social studies
    b. Strong emphasis on reading and science and relatively little emphasis on math and social studies
    c. Strong emphasis on reading and math and relatively little emphasis on science and social studies
    d. Strong emphasis on reading and language arts and relatively little emphasis on math and science

5. Of the following which is the most accurate description of curriculum in middle schools?
    a. Strong emphasis on reading and math and relatively little emphasis on science and social studies
    b. Strong emphasis on making connections among topics and real-world applications
    c. Strong emphasis on individual content areas such as math, science, social studies, and English
    d. Strong emphasis on math and science, moderate emphasis on reading and language arts, and little emphasis on social studies

6. Of the following which is the most accurate description of the curriculum in middle schools compared to the curriculum in junior high schools?
    a. The curriculum in middle schools is more likely to be integrated and focus on real-world problems than is the curriculum in junior high schools.
    b. The curriculum in middle schools is more likely to emphasize reading, language arts, and math than is the curriculum in junior high schools.
    c. The curriculum in middle schools is more likely to emphasize math topics that are advanced for adolescents, such as pre-algebra and algebra than is the curriculum in junior high schools.
    d. The curriculum in middle schools is more likely to be delivered with teacher-centered approaches to instruction, such as lecture, than is the curriculum in junior high schools.

7. Which of the following best illustrates integrated curriculum?
    a. Having students test how quickly different aspirin tablets dissolve and then read an article that describes how quickly different pain relievers begin to work
    b. Having students do word problems in math in which they have to carefully identify what information is given and what information they need to provide
    c. Having students use rulers and protractors to measure the angles and the lengths of sides of triangles
    d. Having students identify art pieces from different historical periods

8. Which of the following best describes the implicit curriculum?
   a.   What students learn in clubs and organizations (such as a science club)
   b.   What students learn through curriculum guides and state standards
   c.   What students learn that is found in their textbooks
   d.   What students learn as communicated by the way teachers interact with them

9. Topics teachers decide to leave out of courses of study are best described as making up which of the following?
   a.   The explicit curriculum
   b.   The implicit curriculum
   c.   The null curriculum
   d.   The missing curriculum

10. Which of the following best describes students who are involved in the extracurriculum (such as sports, clubs, and school plays)?
   a.   Marginal students more often participate in extracurricular activities than do high achievers because these activities help marginal students feel a sense of accomplishment.
   b.   Students who participate in extracurricular activities tend to get lower grades than students who don't participate because time spent in extracurricular activities is taken away from studying.
   c.   Cultural minorities tend to participate in extracurricular activities more than nonminorities because these activities give minorities a feeling of cultural identity.
   d.   Students who participate in extracurricular activities tend to get higher grades and be more motivated than students who don't participate in extracurricular activities.

11. Which of the following best illustrates an activity in the extracurriculum?
   a.   Learning in an environmental science class that global warming is becoming an increasing problem
   b.   Learning lines for your part in *A Man for All Seasons*, the play your class is putting on in the spring
   c.   Practicing your saxophone for your jazz music class
   d.   Trying to increase the number of situps you're able to do in a minute as part of your physical education class

12. Which of the following statements best describes the relationship between extracurricular activities and effective schools?
   a.   A well-developed and comprehensive extracurricular program is one of the characteristics of an effective school.
   b.   Schools that are academically effective de-emphasize extracurricular activities because extracurricular activities tend to detract from the academic orientation of the school.
   c.   Effective schools emphasize extracurricular activities that are academically related (such as an astronomy club or debate team), but they de-emphasize athletics.
   d.   Effective schools for students placed at-risk emphasize extracurricular activities, but effective schools for students who are not at-risk de-emphasize extracurricular activities.

13. Of the following which most influences the curriculum?
   a.   States and local districts
   b.   Professional organizations
   c.   The individual teacher
   d.   Textbooks

14. With respect to the amount of control middle and secondary teachers have over the curriculum, which of the following is the most accurate statement?
   a. Since middle and secondary teachers' class schedules are determined by specified period lengths, these teachers have little or no control over the curriculum.
   b. Since states publish lists of standards that students are expected to meet , middle and secondary teachers have little or no control over the curriculum.
   c. Since most states have statewide assessment tests for students, middle and secondary teachers have little or no control over the curriculum.
   d. Middle and secondary teachers decide the emphasis to place on different topics in the curriculum and the depth to which the topics will be studied, so these teachers have a great deal of control over the curriculum.

15. You are a first-year teacher, and you're in a discussion with a colleague and friend. "These kids need a solid background in as many areas as possible. There's important information that people need to understand in order to get by in the world." "There's too much information," your friend counters. "What these kids really need is the tools to be able to find the information somewhere." You and your friend are in a discussion about curriculum, and of the following your respective views are most strongly influenced by
   a. the textbooks you're each using.
   b. your local district.
   c. state standards.
   d. your personal philosophies.

16. In some of your classes your instructors are likely to encourage you not to depend heavily on textbooks as a basis for making curriculum decisions. If your behavior is consistent with patterns identified by research, which of the following is most likely?
   a. You will follow your instructors' recommendations, and you'll make most of your curriculum decisions on bases other than textbooks.
   b. You will follow your instructors' recommendations during your first year, but you will then revert to using textbooks as an important basis for making curriculum decisions.
   c. You will not follow your instructors' recommendations during your first year, but as you gain teaching experience, you will largely ignore textbooks as a basis for making curriculum decisions.
   d. You will not follow your instructors' recommendations in either your first year or in subsequent years of teaching.

17. If you make decisions about using textbooks on the basis of research examining their effective use, which of the following is your best decision?
   a. Since textbooks are written by experts in the field, you should cover the topics included in them and in the sequence in which they're presented.
   b. You should cover the topics included in the textbooks and supplement those topics with other topics you feel are important.
   c. You should cover some of the topics in detail, de-emphasize or eliminate others, and add topics you feel are important.
   d. You should abandon textbooks completely and generate your own curriculum based on your professional judgment.

18. Reading, writing, and math are the most strongly emphasized areas of the curriculum in elementary schools. Of the following which is the most likely reason for this emphasis?
   a. Reading, writing, and math are the areas in which students are most commonly tested.
   b. Most teachers philosophically believe that reading, writing, and math are the most important areas of the curriculum.
   c. Reading, writing, and particularly math are the curriculum areas elementary teachers most enjoy teaching.
   d. Reading, writing, and math are the areas in which the most hands-on learning activities can be done.

19. The curriculum since the early 1990s included a much stronger emphasis on environmental education than existed before that time. Of the following what is the most likely reason for this increased emphasis?
  a. The federal influence on the curriculum through passage of a specific piece of legislation
  b. The state influence on education through statewide testing in the area of environmental education
  c. The local district influence on the curriculum through the expression of districts' missions
  d. The influence of textbooks on the curriculum because more environmental education textbooks now exist than did before the early 1990s

20. The process of focusing curriculum on predetermined goals or benchmarks that identify the content students should understand and the skills they should have after completing an area of study is best described as
  a. an explicit curriculum.
  b. an implicit curriculum.
  c. content-driven education.
  d. standards-based education.

21. Of the following which statement best describes the way professional organizations (such as the National Council of Teachers of Mathematics) influence curriculum?
  a. Professional organizations publish tests that measure students' understanding of content recommended by the organization.
  b. Professional organizations publish standards that students are expected to meet.
  c. Professional organizations recommend textbooks that then become part of state-adopted textbook lists.
  d. Professional organizations lobby the federal government to try to influence legislation that will support the organizations' goals.

22. State-published documents that typically include standards, learning activities, and performance expectations for students are best described as
  a. curriculum guides.
  b. lesson plans.
  c. explicit curricula.
  d. implicit curricula.

23. Which of the following are arguments supporting a national curriculum?
  (1) Other industrialized countries with high-achieving students (such as Japan) have national standards and national testing.
  (2) A national curriculum would narrow the achievement gap between cultural minorities and nonminorities.
  (3) American society is highly mobile, and a national curriculum would make learners' backgrounds more consistent.
  (4) Standards and levels of achievement vary significantly from state to state.

  a. 1, 2, 3, 4
  b. 1, 2, 3
  c. 1, 3, 4
  d. 2, 3, 4

24. Which of the following are arguments made by opponents of a national curriculum?
   (1) Local school and local district accountability would be weakened.
   (2) A huge federal bureaucracy would be created.
   (3) A national curriculum would not be responsive to the diversity that exists in learners.
   (4) A national curriculum would lower the standards that exist in many states.

    a.   1, 2, 3, 4
    b.   1, 2, 3
    c.   1, 3, 4
    d.   2, 3, 4

25. Research indicates that nearly 70 percent of all school districts in the United States have policies in place to teach sexuality education. Of this 70 percent approximately what fraction teaches that abstinence is the only option outside marriage, and any information about contraception is forbidden (regardless of whether their students are sexually active or at risk of pregnancy or sexually transmitted diseases)?
    a.   One tenth
    b.   One third
    c.   One half
    d.   Two thirds

26. Which of the following is the closest approximation of the percentage of Americans who favor sexuality education and believe that young people should be given information to protect themselves from unplanned pregnancies and sexually transmitted diseases?
    a.   25 percent
    b.   50 percent
    c.   75 percent
    d.   90 percent

27. Which of the following is the most accurate description of the character education versus moral education debate?
    a.   Both agree that education in morality is needed, but they differ primarily in the terminology they use.
    b.   Moral education believes that teaching moral values is necessary (hence the name), whereas character education believes that teaching moral values is not necessary.
    c.   Both agree that education in morality is needed, but they differ in what they believe the goals and methods of instruction should be.
    d.   Moral education believes that the development of morality should focus on groups, whereas character education believes that the development of morality should focus on individuals.

28. Which of the following is *not* a criticism of character education?
    a.   Character education emphasizes indoctrination versus education.
    b.   Character education focuses on behavior instead of understanding.
    c.   Character education overemphasizes thinking at the expense of action.
    d.   Character education doesn't consider transfer of values into behavior.

29. Which of the following is *not* a criticism of moral education?
    a.   Moral education overemphasizes thinking at the expense of behavior.
    b.   Moral education has a relativistic view of morality with no right or wrong answers.
    c.   Moral education deals with issues that are removed from the real world of the classroom.
    d.   Moral education overemphasizes hypothetical versus actual moral issues.

30. Based on public opinion polls, which of the following statements best describes the extent to which people agree on teaching values, such as honesty, democracy, acceptance of people of different races, caring for friends and family, acceptance of homosexuals, and acceptance of a woman's right to choose an abortion.
   a. The public opinion polls overwhelmingly (90% or more in favor) support teaching all the values on the list.
   b. The public opinion polls overwhelmingly (90% or more in favor) support teaching all the values on the list except the acceptance of a woman's right to choose an abortion (about 50% in favor).
   c. The public opinion polls overwhelmingly (90% or more in favor) support teaching all the values on the list except the acceptance of homosexuals and the acceptance of a woman's right to choose an abortion (about 50% in favor of each).
   d. The public opinion polls overwhelmingly (90% or more in favor) support teaching all the values on the list except the acceptance of people of different races, the acceptance of homosexuals, and the acceptance of a woman's right to choose an abortion (about 50% in favor of each).

31. Of the following which best describes the goal of service learning (involving students in social service projects)?
   a. To clarify the implicit curriculum for all learners
   b. To expand the extracurriculum to involve more students placed at-risk
   c. To make all students more socially responsible
   d. To meet state standards for improved environmental education

32. Of the following which is the best description of *creationism*?
   a. The belief that all the events in the universe exist in a predetermined sequence
   b. The belief that the existence of the universe and all its parts is the result of work done by God
   c. The belief that the organisms that exist on the earth at a certain time are the result of environmental conditions
   d. The belief that the most righteous people on earth will have eternal life and the less righteous will not

33. Of the following which is the best description of *evolution*?
   a. A theory suggesting that all living things change in response to environmental conditions
   b. A theory suggesting that all organisms and events in the world change in response to a predetermined sequence
   c. A theory suggesting that changes in living things are the result of work done by God
   d. A theory suggesting that organisms evolve because of the will of a supreme being

34. Which of the following is the best description of *censorship*?
   a. The process of determining what knowledge students should have and what skills they should possess after completing a course of study
   b. The process of requiring teachers to follow the specifications outlined in curriculum guides
   c. The process of removing students from school for engaging in lewd or immoral behavior
   d. The process of not allowing the use of certain books in the school curriculum

Items for Analysis and Critical Thinking

Use the following information for Items 35 and 36:

You believe that learning to write persuasive essays is essential for students. You also believe that the only way that they'll learn to write them effectively is with a great deal of practice. To begin, you display two sample persuasive essays on the overhead, one that is well written and one that isn't. In a discussion you help students understand the characteristics of an effective persuasive essay.

35. Of the following which are curriculum decisions?
   (1) You believe that learning to write persuasive essays is essential for students.
   (2) You believe that the only way that they'll learn to write them effectively is with a great deal of practice.
   (3) You display two sample persuasive essays on the overhead, one that is well written and one that isn't.
   (4) In a discussion you help students understand the characteristics of an effective persuasive essay.

   a. 1, 2, 3
   b. 1
   c. 1, 2
   d. 2, 3

36. Of the following which are decisions about instruction?
   (1) You believe that learning to write persuasive essays is essential for students.
   (2) You believe that the only way that they'll learn to write them effectively is with a great deal of practice.
   (3) You display two sample persuasive essays on the overhead, one that is well written and one that isn't.
   (4) In a discussion you help students understand the characteristics of an effective persuasive essay.

   a. 2, 3, 4
   b. 3, 4
   c. 2, 4
   d. 4

37. Whenever Calvin Green's students are unable to answer in question-and-answer sessions, he prompts them until they can give an acceptable answer. "I want them to learn that being uncertain is all a part of the learning process," Calvin explains. Learning that "being uncertain is all part of the learning process" best illustrates the
   a. explicit curriculum.
   b. implicit curriculum.
   c. extracurriculum.
   d. integrated curriculum.

Use the following information for Items 38–40:

Anya Kuertan, an eighth-grade American history teacher, teaches a week-long unit on the American Civil War. She emphasizes the relationships between the fact that the North was industrial and the South was more agricultural and the geography of the two parts of the country. She also relates these factors to the causes of the war, the relative advantages of the North and the South, and the war's outcomes. Anya is animated in her discussions of the topic, and her own interest in it is obvious. She also emphasizes that all the students have a right to express their opinions and conclusions about the topic as they study it.

  As she reflects on her unit, she concludes, "The next time I teach it, I need to put more emphasis on the human side of the issues, slavery and racism, the suffering of the people in the North and the South, and the bitterness that was left in the wake of the war."

38. Which of the following best describes Anya's emphasis on the relationships among industry, agriculture, geography, and the causes and outcomes of the war?
   a. That makes up the explicit curriculum.
   b. That makes up the implicit curriculum.
   c. That makes up the focused curriculum.
   d. That makes up the null curriculum.

39. Which of the following best describes Anya's enthusiasm and her emphasis on all students having the right to express opinions and conclusions?
   a. That makes up the explicit curriculum.
   b. That makes up the implicit curriculum.
   c. That makes up the focused curriculum.
   d. That makes up the null curriculum.

40. Which of the following best describes Anya's lack of emphasis, this time, on the human side of the issues and other topics, such as slavery, suffering, and bitterness after the war?
    a.   That makes up the explicit curriculum.
    b.   That makes up the implicit curriculum.
    c.   That makes up the missing curriculum.
    d.   That makes up the null curriculum.

Use the following information for Items 41–44:

"What are you studying in geometry?" Jeff Trump asks Gabriella Suarez, one of the students in his chemistry class. "We're studying theorems that we use to prove that triangles are congruent," she responds. "I was confused at first, but now I'm catching on, and I have a *B* for this 9 weeks."

Janet Wilson, a science teacher, strongly emphasizes integration of her math topics with science topics, and she regularly works with Joe Nagel, the math teacher on her team, to try to meet these goals. For example, when Janet's students study genetics, Joe has them calculate the proportions and percentages of students who have blue eyes compared to those that have brown or green eyes.

Rosano Ramos makes a strong attempt to integrate her science topics with language arts, which she emphasizes by spending about an hour a day on it. For example, she recently had the students read stories about different animals and the way they adapted to their environments, and then she had the students make oral reports on what they had read.

David Nalbandian, a life science teacher, sees that Jeremy Smith, one of his students, is having difficulty in his class. He asks Jeremy who his English teacher is, and after school he sends an e-mail to Jeremy's English teacher, asking if they could meet for a few minutes to talk about Jeremy's performance in English.

41. Based on the curriculum information above, the teacher who most likely teaches in an elementary school is
    a.   Jeff.
    b.   Janet.
    c.   Rosano.
    d.   David.

42. Based on the curriculum information above, the teacher who most likely teaches in a middle school is
    a.   Jeff.
    b.   Janet.
    c.   Rosano.
    d.   David.

43. Based on the curriculum information above, the teacher who most likely teaches in a junior high is
    a.   Jeff.
    b.   Janet.
    c.   Rosano.
    d.   David.

44. Based on the curriculum information above, the teacher who most likely teaches in a high school is
    a.   Jeff.
    b.   Janet.
    c.   Rosano.
    d.   David.

45. Your school district, concerned about issues such as teen pregnancy and sexually transmitted diseases, wants to create and implement a sex education course as part of the schools' health curricula. A parent group sues, contending that sex education is outside the scope of the public school curriculum. If resolution of this case is consistent with other cases involving sex education, which of the following is the most likely outcome?

    a.   Your district's right to create a sex education curriculum will be held up in court, and parents who object will be free to remove their children from attendance.

    b.   Your district's right to create a sex education curriculum will be held up in court, and all students will be required to attend.

    c.   Your district's right to create a sex education curriculum will be held up in court, and parents who object will be free to remove their children from attendance if they can demonstrate that the curriculum is a violation of their religious beliefs.

    d.   Your district's right to create a sex education curriculum will be turned down by the courts on the grounds that schools must be responsive to the wishes of parents in curriculum issues that are controversial.

Use the following information for Items 46 and 47:

Four teachers were discussing the issue of teaching morals and values in schools. Jennifer commented, "We shouldn't be teaching values in the schools. Values and morals should be learned in the home or the church."

      "That's naive," Isabelle countered. "We teach values whenever we work with our kids. And if we don't teach some values, like honesty, they'll never get them any other place. We should work on values and reinforce them."

      "All that stuff is bogus," Adam retorted. "You can't teach values or morals. The values the kids have are the ones they are either born with or learn before they're 5 years old. What we should be doing is focusing on the rules we've set up and trying to be fair to everybody. Then values take care of themselves."

      "I agree with you, Isabelle, up to a point," Cal responded. "We need to do some work with morals, but I'm not comfortable with deciding for the kids what values they ought to have. I think we should have some serious discussions with the kids and help them learn to understand their own values."

46. The teacher whose position is most closely aligned with character education is

    a.   Jennifer
    b.   Isabelle
    c.   Adam
    d.   Cal

47. The teacher whose position is most closely aligned with moral education is

    a.   Jennifer
    b.   Isabelle
    c.   Adam
    d.   Cal

48. Your state has implemented a 60-hour service-learning component that all students must complete before they will be allowed to graduate from high school. A parent group has protested and has challenged the legality of the requirement in court. If resolution of this case is consistent with other cases involving service-learning requirements, which of the following is the most likely outcome?

    a.   Your state's right to require a service-learning component will be held up in court, based on the argument that service-learning courses promote citizenship and social responsibility.

    b.   Your state's right to require a service-learning component will be held up in court, based on the argument that curriculum decisions have been placed in the hands of states and all reasonable curricula can be offered.

    c.   Your state's right to require a service-learning component will be turned down by the courts, arguing that an effective rationale for requiring service-learning cannot be made.

    d.   Your state's right to require a service-learning component will be turned down by the courts, arguing that service-learning is technically an extracurricular activity and participation in extracurricular activities cannot be required.

Extended-Response Items

49. Describe the controversy involved in integrating curriculum. What does research indicate about the effectiveness of integrating curriculum (compared to not integrating curriculum) for increasing student learning? (6 points)

50. Describe research that has examined the impact of participating in sports. Include its impact on both boys and girls. (4 points)

51. Describe and explain three ways in which states influence curriculum. (6 points)

52. Describe outcomes-based education, and explain the controversy involved in it. (4 points)

53. Three common features exist in suggested curriculum reforms in all content areas (such as science, math, or social studies). Describe and explain these features. (6 points)

54. Describe and explain the controversy involved in textbook censorship. Include both sides of the issue in your response, and describe typical court responses in legal cases involving censorship. (6 points)

55. Describe and explain the controversy involved in the representation of women and cultural minorities in the curriculum. Include both sides of the issue in your response, and relate the history that has led to the controversy. (6 points)

CHAPTER ELEVEN

INSTRUCTION IN AMERICAN CLASSROOMS

Knowledge-Level Items

1. Which of the following statements best describes the teacher effectiveness research?
   a. The body of knowledge describing differences in the behavior of teachers of high-achieving students compared to that of teachers of lower-achieving students
   b. The body of knowledge describing differences in the beliefs of teachers about their abilities to promote learning in all students regardless of their backgrounds
   c. The body of knowledge describing teachers' willingness to invest time in the protection and development of young people
   d. The body of knowledge that examines the extent to which teachers behave in ways they would like their students to imitate

2. Of the following what is the best description of effective learning goals?
   a. Activities teachers design to promote learning
   b. Techniques teachers use to help students learn
   c. Knowledge and skills teachers will use to increase learning
   d. Knowledge or skills students are expected to acquire

3. In today's classrooms teachers' goals most commonly focus on which cell of the taxonomy for learning, teaching, and assessing?
   a. The cell where *factual knowledge* intersects with the cognitive process *remember*
   b. The cell where *procedural knowledge* intersects with the cognitive process *apply*
   c. The cell where *metacognitive knowledge* intersects with the cognitive process *create*
   d. The cell where *conceptual knowledge* intersects with the cognitive process *understand*

4. Which of the following statements best describes instructional alignment?
   a. Teachers' beliefs about their abilities to instruct students in such a way that all students, regardless of ability, will learn as much as possible
   b. The consistency between teachers' goals, learning activities, practice they provide for students, and assessment
   c. Teachers' willingness to invest their time and effort to be sure that all students learn as much as possible
   d. Teachers' behaviors that cause students to behave in ways that mirror the teachers' behaviors

5. When teachers' lessons are out of alignment, which of the following is the most likely reason?
   a. Teachers' thinking about their learning goals isn't clear.
   b. Teachers are low in personal teaching efficacy.
   c. Teachers are unprofessional.
   d. Teachers lack essential teaching skills, such as the ability to guide students with questioning.

6. When a teacher believes he or she can positively affect student learning, that teacher is said to possess
   a. effective attitudes.
   b. teaching efficacy.
   c. empathetic effectiveness.
   d. proactive facilitation.

7. Of the following the most effective way to communicate caring to students is to
   a. smile at them frequently.
   b. compliment them on personal characteristics.
   c. spend time with them.
   d. be enthusiastic in class.

91

8. Which of the following is *not* considered to be a characteristic of a caring teacher?
    a. Showing respect and politeness to all students
    b. Praising students whether or not they try
    c. Helping with personal problems
    d. Valuing individuality

9. Which of the following statements most precisely describes modeling?
    a. Teaching in ways that result in students achieving more than would be expected for their backgrounds and ability levels
    b. Believing that you're able to get all students to learn regardless of their backgrounds and ability levels
    c. Being willing to invest time in the protection and development of young people
    d. Behaving in ways that you would like students to imitate

10. As a teacher you treat your students with courtesy and respect, and you demonstrate—in such a way that they can see—that you study and work hard. Of the following your behavior best illustrates
    a. high personal teaching efficacy.
    b. caring.
    c. enthusiasm.
    d. modeling.

11. Of the following which is the best way to demonstrate enthusiasm about the content you're teaching?
    a. Smile frequently as you explain the content to your students
    b. Make statements such as, "I'm really enthusiastic about this lesson," whether or not you really like the topic
    c. Demonstrate your own genuine personal interest in the content
    d. Allow all students who raise their hands to answer as many questions as they want

12. Research indicates that teachers call on some students more often than others, give them more time to answer, and prompt them more when the students are originally unable to answer. Which of the following best describes why teachers treat the students differently?
    a. They care more about the favored students (the ones they call on more, give more time to answer, and prompt more) than about the ones less favored.
    b. They are better models for the favored students (the ones they call on more, etc.) than they are for the ones less favored.
    c. They have higher expectations for the favored students (the ones they call on more, etc.) than the ones less favored.
    d. They are more enthusiastic about working with the favored students (the ones they call on more, etc.) than they are about working with the less favored students.

13. A math teacher displays a word problem on the overhead, asks, "What is the first thing we should do in this problem?" pauses briefly, and then says, "Calvin?" as she calls on one of the students in the class. This brief episode best illustrates which of the following?
    a. Teacher expectations
    b. Teacher modeling
    c. A teacher's demonstration of enthusiasm
    d. A teacher's demonstration of wait-time

14. The set of teacher actions that maximizes the amount of time available for instruction is best described as
    a. modeling.
    b. organization.
    c. expectations.
    d. personal teaching efficacy.

15. A lesson in which all parts of a teacher's instruction are related and lead to a specific point is best described as
    a. a focused lesson.
    b. a modeled lesson.
    c. a formative lesson.
    d. a thematic lesson.

16. Information students are given about their current understanding that can be used to increase future learning is best described as
    a. feedback.
    b. personal efficacy.
    c. expectations.
    d. wait-time.

17. Of the following which is teachers' primary concern as they anticipate their first jobs?
    a. Their inability to motivate students
    b. Their inability to effectively explain topics to students
    c. Their lack of understanding of the content they're teaching
    d. Their inability to create and maintain orderly classrooms

18. Which of the following statements best describes the relationship between classroom management and effective instruction?
    a. Classroom management is a prerequisite to effective instruction; order must first be established before teachers can instruct effectively.
    b. Orderly classrooms are a result or an outcome of effective instruction; if instruction is effective, classroom management takes care of itself.
    c. Classroom management and effective instruction are interdependent; it is virtually impossible to teach effectively in a chaotic classroom, and orderly classrooms are virtually impossible if instruction is ineffective.
    d. Classroom management and effective instruction are not related; classroom management refers to students' behaviors, and effective instruction refers to teachers' behaviors.

19. Which of the following statements best describes the difference between classroom procedures and classroom rules?
    a. Students are often reinforced for following classroom rules, but they aren't reinforced for following classroom procedures.
    b. Classroom procedures describe acceptable behaviors, whereas classroom rules describe unacceptable behaviors.
    c. Classroom procedures describe routines to be followed, whereas classroom rules describe standards for acceptable behavior.
    d. Classroom procedures focus on a management approach to developing an orderly classroom, whereas classroom rules focus on a discipline approach to developing an orderly classroom.

20. Which of the following are examples of assessment?
    (1) Listening to a student's answer to a question
    (2) Looking at students' responses to a homework assignment
    (3) Checking students' answers to items on a quiz
    (4) Watching students as they work on a lab activity

    a. 1, 2, 3, 4
    b. 1, 4
    c. 1, 2, 3
    d. 3

21. Alternative assessments that directly measure students' skills and understanding in a lifelike setting are best described as

    a.   portfolios.
    b.   direct assessments.
    c.   reliable assessments.
    d.   performance assessments.

22. Collections of work that are reviewed against preset criteria in order to judge a student's progress over time are called

    a.   checklists.
    b.   portfolios.
    c.   feedback.
    d.   objective assessments.

23. Which of the following is the most valid description of learning from a behaviorist point of view?

    a.   Sensations paired together enough times that they become associated
    b.   Increases in behavior as a result of anticipating desirable consequences
    c.   Changes in behavior as a result of observing similar behaviors in others
    d.   Changes in observable behavior occurring as a result of experience

24. For which of the following goals is a behaviorist approach to learning most appropriate?

    a.   To understand the characteristics of an effective persuasive essay in English
    b.   To understand the relationships between the concepts *force* and *work* in science
    c.   To be able to find the longitude and latitude of different American cities in geography
    d.   To know math facts such as 7 x 8 = and 12 x 6 =

25. Of the following which is the primary problem with behaviorism as a basis for guiding learning?

    a.   Behaviorism treats learners as if they're passive; they change their behavior in response to reinforcers and punishers.
    b.   Using reinforcers and punishers with students doesn't produce changes in behavior; students don't learn when behaviorism is used as a basis for instruction.
    c.   Learners resent being subjected to reinforcers and punishers; behaviorism results in a decrease in student motivation.
    d.   Behaviorism reduces teachers' personal efficacy; they don't believe they can get all students to learn when behaviorism is used as a basis for instruction.

26. Which of the following statements best describes the basic principle on which cognitive learning theory is based?

    a.   Learners' behaviors increase when they're rewarded for demonstrating the behaviors (and decrease when the behaviors aren't rewarded).
    b.   Learning does not result in a change in behavior (it changes only mental processes).
    c.   Learners are mentally active (rather than passive).
    d.   Learners are innately motivated to seek feedback about their learning (and change their understanding based on the feedback).

27. Many people believe that the earth is closer to the sun in June (summer in the Northern Hemisphere) than it is in December, in spite of the fact that they're taught that the earth is slightly farther away from the sun in June. Of the following which is the best explanation for this belief?

    a.   The people haven't been adequately reinforced by teachers for having the correct belief.
    b.   The people construct the belief that the earth is closer to the sun in June because it makes more sense to them.
    c.   The people responded passively to the instruction about the earth, sun, and seasons when they were students in schools.
    d.   The people were taught by teachers with low personal teaching efficacy, so the teachers didn't believe that the people were capable of the correct understanding when the people were students in schools.

28. Consider instruction based on behaviorist views of learning compared to cognitive views of learning. Which of the following is the most accurate statement?
   a. The goals of instruction will always be different when instruction is based on behaviorism as compared to cognitive views of learning, so the learning activities will also be different.
   b. Instruction based on behaviorism is more sophisticated and demanding for teachers than is instruction based on cognitive views of learning, so teachers using behaviorism as a basis for instruction will need to be more knowledgeable.
   c. The goals of instruction will, or can be, the same when using either behaviorism or cognitive views of learning as a basis for instruction, but the approaches to instruction will be very different.
   d. Assessment is an important part of instruction when it is based on behaviorism, but assessment isn't a part of instruction when based on cognitive views of learning (since learning doesn't always result in changes in observable behavior).

29. Suppose a teacher identifies a specific goal, arranges information so that patterns can be found, and then guides students to the goal. This approach to instruction is best described as
   a. cooperative learning.
   b. cognitive learning.
   c. behaviorist learning.
   d. discovery learning.

30. In schools where the achievement gap between cultural minorities and nonminorities is narrowing, which of the following are prominent?
   (1) The belief by the school leadership that all students can and will learn
   (2) Specific and demanding goals
   (3) Instruction that focuses on specific explanations by teachers and attentive listening by students
   (4) Regular and thorough assessment of student progress

   a. 1, 2, 3, 4
   b. 1, 2, 3
   c. 1, 2, 4
   d. 2, 3

Items for Analysis and Critical Thinking

31. A teacher wants her students to be able to identify examples of adjectives and adverbs in the context of a written paragraph. Of the following the most accurate classification of this objective in the taxonomy for learning, teaching and assessing is
   a. the cell where *factual knowledge* intersects with the cognitive process *remember*.
   b. the cell where *procedural knowledge* intersects with the cognitive process *apply*.
   c. the cell where *metacognitive knowledge* intersects with the cognitive process *create*.
   d. the cell where *conceptual knowledge* intersects with the cognitive process *understand*.

32. Rodnaie Rixley was reflecting on the problem of Luiz. He was in her third period English class, and he was failing. She had tried gentle reminders to encourage him to complete his work and made sure she recognized him when he did so; she had tried simplifying directions; she had tried counseling him; she had tried drawing him out in class and elaborating on his comments and questions. "So far, none of those has really worked for very long," she mused, "but I know I can get him to learn. I wonder what I should try next. I think I'll call his parents and ask for their help." Which of the following statements best describes Rodnaie's behavior in this episode?
   a. She has demonstrated high personal teaching efficacy.
   b. She has demonstrated modeling and vicarious learning.
   c. She has demonstrated effective organizational skills.
   d. She has demonstrated a commitment to ethnic diversity.

33. Sally Harvey, an eighth-grade math teacher, typically spends about 7 minutes after the bell rings taking roll, handing out papers, and writing assignments on the board. Karen Walters, who teaches in the room next to Sally, writes her assignments on the board during the time the students are moving from one class to another. Based on this information, which of the following conclusions is most valid?

    a.   Sally is a more caring teacher than is Karen.
    b.   Sally has higher personal teaching efficacy than does Karen.
    c.   Karen is better organized than is Sally.
    d.   Karen is a more effective teacher than is Sally.

34. Look at the following teacher statement: "This grammar lesson will help . . . will help us get to where we understand . . . uh, know how to use the active voice in our writing. Before we start . . . we want to first review . . . let's look at what we did for today." Of the following features related to teaching strategies, this example best illustrates ineffective

    a.   modeling.
    b.   organization.
    c.   review.
    d.   communication.

35. A teacher comments to her students, "All right, everyone, we're finished with our discussion of animals that have radial symmetry, and we're now going to look at those with bilateral symmetry." Of the following her comment best illustrates

    a.   a classroom procedure.
    b.   a form of modeling.
    c.   a thematic lesson.
    d.   a transition signal.

36. You catch Devon, one of your more energetic students, running past you in the school hallway, which is against the rules. You stop him and say, "Devon, explain to me why running in the hallways is against the rules." He hesitantly responds, "Because someone could get hurt when we run." "Good," you reply. "Now, walk back to the end of the hallway, and then walk back past me to wherever you're going." Of the following which best explains your action?

    a.   You are applying an obedience model of classroom management since you caught Devon in the act of running and stopped him.
    b.   You are applying a responsibility model of classroom management since you helped Devon understand the reason for the rule, and you applied a logical consequence (you made him go back and walk).
    c.   You are applying an obedience model of classroom management since you forced Devon to walk back to the end of the hall, turn around, and walk back.
    d.   You are applying a responsibility model of classroom management since Devon could see that you were responsible for being sure that all the students in the school's hallways were safe.

37. "You can't get away with anything in here," Crystal whispers to Sarah. "Mrs. Marquez always knows what's going on." The concept best illustrated in this advice is

    a.   classroom management.
    b.   teacher discipline.
    c.   teacher organization.
    d.   teacher withitness.

Read the following case study. Then refer to it to answer Items 38–48.

CASE STUDY: LA-JUAN HAWKINS' EIGHTH-GRADE SCIENCE LESSON

(1) La-Juan Hawkins, a first-year teacher, has had her science students studying the structure of the atom, and she now wants them to understand static electricity.
(2) "Did you finish your homework?" Jay asks Patricia as they walk into the classroom.
(3) "Are you kidding? You miss a homework assignment in this class and you're a dead duck," Amy interjects.

(4) "Boy, Mrs. Hawkins, you had my whole family on the ropes last night. I had both my mom and dad helping me find examples of the elements you assigned us," Ken comments as he comes into class.

(5) "That's good for you," La-Juan smiles back. "I know it was a tough assignment, but it makes us think. And I know all of you in here can understand this stuff if I teach it well enough, and you study hard enough."

(6) La-Juan begins, "We've been talking about elements. Let's see what we remember. Look at the model." She holds up a model that has three balls of red clay with +'s on them to represent protons and three balls of yellow clay with 0's on them to represent neutrons. "What element does this represent? . . . Allen?"

(7) ". . . Lithium," Allen responds.

(8) "Good, and how do we know, . . . Kathleen?"

(9) "There are three protons in there," Kathleen responds pointing to the model.

(10) "All right! Very good.

(11) "Now," she says. "Let's think about electrons. . . . What do we know about them? . . . Peter?" she asks, seeing Peter staring intently at the clay pieces in her hand.

(12) "They're . . . out there," Peter responds, moving his hands to demonstrate that the electrons are outside the nucleus.

(13) "Yes, good. We said that the electrons are in orbit around the nucleus," La-Juan nods.

(14) "And are they tightly or loosely attracted to the nucleus? . . . Janice?"

(15) ". . . Sort of loosely, I think," Janice tentatively responds.

(16) "Yes, very good, Janice. We can 'scrape' electrons off," La-Juan continues, "so they're loosely attached. Now, keep that in mind because it's important. We can get electrons off the atoms fairly easily with heat or even by simply rubbing them, while the nucleus is very hard to break up.

(17) "Now, let's take a look," La-Juan says as she steps quickly over to her file cabinet and takes out an inflated balloon and a wool sweater. "Watch." She then rubs the balloon vigorously with the sweater, steps over and puts the balloon near Michelle's hair and asks, "What do you notice here? . . . Vicki?"

(18) "The balloon is making Michelle's hair stick up," Vicki responds to the giggles of the class.

(19) "Yes!" La-Juan smiles. "Now, what we want to try and do today is figure out why this happened.

(20) ". . . Look again," she continues when she sees them all looking at her. She then takes another inflated balloon, holds it against the chalkboard, and lets it go. "What happened here? . . . Joe?"

(21) "It just fell down," Joe shrugs.

(22) "Let's try it again," La-Juan continues as she rubs the balloon on the sweater.

(23) "Now what? . . . Melody?"

(24) "It's stuck up there now."

(25) "Yes, it is! Now, this is a little tough, but I'll bet we can figure out why it stuck this time. Give it a try, John?"

(26) ". . . Well, you rubbed it on the sweater the second time."

(27) "And, what did the rubbing do? . . . Tracey?

(28) ". . ."

(29) "Think about the electrons," La-Juan encourages.

(30) ". . . Well, some of the electrons might have been rubbed off the sweater," Tracey responds uncertainly.

(31) "Yes, exactly, Tracey. They're bound tighter in the balloon, so the balloon collects them from the sweater.

(32) "So now what do we have? Randy?"

(33) ". . . We have more electrons than protons on the balloon."

(34) "Bravo! Excellent thinking. So then what? . . . Ed?"

(35) ". . . The extra electrons attracted Michelle's hair."

(36) "And what else? . . . Carol?"

(37) "The same thing happened to the board."

(38) La-Juan then has the students explain additional examples, such as why clothes stick together in the dryer and why people sometimes get a shock after they walk across a carpet and touch a door knob.

38. Look at paragraphs 3–4 in the case study. Of the following they best illustrate La-Juan's
    a. personal teaching efficacy.
    b. caring.
    c. expectations.
    d. modeling and enthusiasm.

39. Look at paragraph 5 in the case study. Of the following it best illustrates La-Juan's
    a. personal teaching efficacy.
    b. enthusiasm.
    c. instructional alignment.
    d. effective classroom management.

40. Of the following the paragraph that best illustrates La-Juan's use of emphasis is
    a. 5
    b. 11
    c. 16
    d. 25

41. Look at paragraphs 6, 8, 11, 14, 17, 20, 23, and 27 of the case study. Of the following they best illustrate
    a. La-Juan's high personal teaching efficacy.
    b. La-Juan's high expectations for students.
    c. La-Juan's equitable distribution of questions.
    d. La-Juan's effective classroom management.

42. Look at paragraphs 6 and 17 in the case study. Of the following they best illustrate La-Juan's
    a. high personal teaching efficacy.
    b. high expectations.
    c. effective modeling.
    d. effective presentation of subject matter.

43. Of the following the paragraph that best illustrates La-Juan's use of an example is
    a. 4
    b. 16
    c. 17
    d. 30

44. Consider the questions La-Juan asked in paragraphs 6, 8, 11, and 14. Which of the following is the most accurate statement?
    a. All four of the questions are high level.
    b. All four of the questions are low level.
    c. The questions in paragraphs 6 and 8 are high level, and the questions in 11 and 14 are low level.
    d. The questions in paragraphs 6, 11, and 14 are low level, and the question in paragraph 8 is high level.

45. Consider again the questions La-Juan asked in paragraphs 6, 8, 11, and 14. Which of the following is the best assessment of the questions?
    a. All the questions were effective since they were all high level.
    b. None of the questions were effective since they were all low level.
    c. The high-level question(s) was(were) effective, but the low-level question(s) was(were) not.
    d. All the questions were effective because they all led the students to La-Juan's goal.

46. Look at paragraph 31 in the lesson. Of the following it best illustrates
    a. La-Juan's attempt to be an effective model for her students.
    b. La-Juan's attempt to provide Tracey with feedback about her understanding.
    c. La-Juan's caring.
    d. La-Juan's equitable distribution of questions.

47. Look at paragraphs 27–29. Of the following they best illustrate La-Juan's
    a. personal teaching efficacy.
    b. clear communication.
    c. effective organization.
    d. effective prompting.

48. Look at paragraph 38 in the lesson. Of the following it best illustrates La-Juan's
   a. high personal teaching efficacy.
   b. high expectations.
   c. attempt to provide students with feedback.
   d. attempt to assess her students' understanding.

Extended-Response Items

49. Write an analysis of the effectiveness of different levels (high-level versus low-level) of questions. In your analysis first discuss whether one is more effective than the other, and if so, when or under what conditions is one more effective than the other. Include in your analysis a discussion of how teachers decide which level of question to ask. (5 points)

50. Look at the case study illustrating La-Juan Hawkins' lesson with her students. Assess the instructional alignment in La-Juan's lesson, that is, was La-Juan's instruction aligned? Include evidence from the case study to support your assessment. (6 points)

51. Look again at the case study illustrating La-Juan Hawkins' lesson with her students. Assess the effectiveness of La-Juan's questioning in the lesson, and include evidence from the case study to support your assessment. (8 points)

52. Look again at the case study illustrating La-Juan Hawkins' lesson with her students. Assess the effectiveness of La-Juan's presentation of subject matter, and include evidence from the case study to support your assessment. (4 points)

53. Describe learning from a behaviorist point of view, and illustrate your description with a specific example. (4 points)

54. Describe learning from a cognitive point of view, and illustrate your description with a specific example. (4 points)

55. Describe the difference between teacher-centered and learner-centered instruction. Then describe the controversy involved in the two approaches, including the criticisms of each. (6 points)

CHAPTER TWELVE

TECHNOLOGY IN AMERICAN SCHOOLS

Knowledge-Level Items

1. Which of the following are forms of technology?
   (1) Computers
   (2) DVD players
   (3) PowerPoint presentations
   (4) The chalkboard

      a. 1, 2, 3, 4
      b. 1, 2, 3
      c. 1, 2
      d. 1, 3

2. Which of the following best illustrates a hardware view of technology?
      a. A teacher displays transparencies on an overhead projector because the transparency illustrates all the parts of an insect in detailed color.
      b. A teacher has students do drill-and-practice activities on the computer because they're more motivated when they work on the computer than they are when she uses flashcards.
      c. A teacher helps students learn how to conduct Internet searches so that they're able to use the Internet to access information.
      d. A teacher has students practice word processing so they'll be able to use computers to improve the efficiency of their writing.

3. Which of the following best illustrates a process view of technology?
      a. A teacher displays transparencies on an overhead projector because the transparency illustrates all the parts of an insect in detailed color.
      b. A teacher uses a videodisc that contains a wide variety of animals to show students examples of birds indigenous to their area.
      c. A teacher uses a PowerPoint presentation to illustrate different examples of plane figures (such as trapezoids and rhombuses) .
      d. A teacher helps students learn how to conduct Internet searches so that they're able to use the Internet to access information.

4. Which of the following best describes the relationships between a hardware view and a process view of technology?
      a. Both are grounded in a transmission view of learning; the teacher is in control of the learning activity, and the technology helps transmit the information to be learned to the students.
      b. Both are grounded in a cognitive-constructivist view of learning, which assumes that students will actively participate in learning activities.
      c. The hardware view is grounded in a transmission view of learning, whereas the process view is more nearly grounded in a cognitive-constructivist view of learning.
      d. The hardware view is not grounded in learning theory, whereas the process view is grounded in a cognitive-constructivist view of learning.

5. Which of the following best describes the thinking of experts with respect to the definition of technology?
      a. Most experts view technology as primarily hardware, such as computers, laserdiscs, and videotapes.
      b. Most experts view technology as primarily a process (such as learning to use computers as a tool to make writing more efficient), and hardware is a tool designed to enhance the process.
      c. Most experts view technology as a combination of hardware and process, with the parts complementing each other.
      d. Experts disagree on a definition of technology, with some holding a hardware view and others retaining a process view.

6. Which of the following best illustrates the use of technology to support instruction?
   a. Students create a database that includes books they've read, their hobbies, and favorite forms of recreation.
   b. Students practice math facts using a computer-based drill-and-practice program.
   c. A teacher puts all her students' quiz, test, and homework scores on a spreadsheet.
   d. A teacher has all her students' names, addresses, and phone numbers in a database that she can quickly access if she needs to contact a parent.

7. "Programs written in a computer language" best describes which of the following?
   a. Software
   b. Tutorials
   c. Hypermedia
   d. Icons

8. Which of the following best describes the relationship between drill-and-practice software and tutorials.
   a. Drill-and-practice programs focus on isolated facts, whereas tutorials deliver an entire integrated instructional sequence.
   b. Drill-and-practice programs support teachers' instruction, whereas tutorials are forms of assistive technology.
   c. Drill-and-practice programs are technology tools, whereas tutorials support teachers' instruction.
   d. Drill-and-practice programs and tutorials are both intended to take the place of teachers over long periods of time.

9. Which of the following are advantages of drill-and-practice programs?
   (1) They immediately tell students what they've mastered and what they need more work on.
   (2) They promote deep understanding of the topics they present.
   (3) They are often motivating for students turned off by paper-and-pencil exercises.
   (4) They save teachers time since teachers don't have to present the information and score students' responses.

   a. 1, 2, 3, 4
   b. 1, 3, 4
   c. 2, 3, 4
   d. 3, 4

10. Pictures that serve as symbols for some action or item in technology are called
    a. software.
    b. icons.
    c. databases.
    d. spreadsheets.

11. Linked forms of technology (such as combining scenarios, pictures, video clips, and laserdisc episodes) are called
    a. spreadsheets.
    b. tutorials.
    c. software.
    d. hypermedia.

12. Of the following what is the primary disadvantage of using technology to support instruction?
    a. Problem solving is an important learning goal, and technology can't be used to teach problem solving.
    b. The novelty of technology has worn off for students, and software must be ever more "glitzy" to maintain students' attention.
    c. The quality of software varies dramatically, and the available software may not be aligned with teachers' goals.
    d. Evidence doesn't exist that current software increases learning, particularly for low-SES students and learners with exceptionalities.

13. Software that uses computers to deliver instructional sequences similar to a teacher's instruction on a topic is best described as
    a. drill-and-practice programs.
    b. hypermedia.
    c. icons.
    d. tutorials.

14. Which of the following statements best describes the key factor that makes tutorials effective?
    a. The quality of the software is the key factor determining how effective a tutorial will be.
    b. The quality of the interactions between the technology and the learner is the key factor determining how effective a tutorial will be.
    c. The level of the requirements for the learner (high-level thinking versus memorization) is the key factor determining how effective a tutorial will be.
    d. The topics students learn when working on the tutorial are the key factor determining how effective a tutorial will be.

15. Of the following which statement best describes the most common criticism of tutorials?
    a. They focus too much on memorized information instead of thinking and application of information.
    b. They are poorly written, so students have difficulty following the directions of the tutorials.
    c. The content is written at too high a level, so teachers are required to supplement them with their own instruction to achieve more meaningful learning goals.
    d. They don't provide enough focus on basic skills, such as reading, writing, and math, so the content learned is peripheral to the main focus of the curriculum.

16. Forms of software that model a real or imaginary system in order to help students understand the system are called
    a. problem-based learning systems.
    b. databases.
    c. hypermedia.
    d. simulations.

17. The ability to involve students in complex, realistic learning activities that are usually unavailable in classrooms best describes an important use of which of the following?
    a. Tutorials
    b. Simulations
    c. Databases
    d. Hypermedia

18. Which of the following are ways in which word processing can be used to improve students' writing?
    (1) It removes the teacher from the process, so teachers don't have to spend time teaching writing.
    (2) It makes entering, revising, and editing text easier, so students are inclined to write more.
    (3) It makes existing text more legible, so the process of revising is less cumbersome.
    (4) It facilitates communication between developing writers through e-mail.

    a. 1, 2, 3, 4
    b. 1, 2, 3
    c. 2, 3, 4
    d. 1, 3, 4

19. Computer programs that allow users to store, organize, and manipulate both text and numerical information are called
    a. tutorials.
    b. spreadsheets.
    c. databases.
    d. the Internet.

20. Computer programs that organize and manipulate numerical data are called
    a. drill-and-practice programs.
    b. tutorials.
    c. spreadsheets.
    d. databases.

21. Which of the following best describes interconnections between computers that allow large numbers of people to communicate and share information worldwide?
    a. The Internet
    b. Assistive technology
    c. Hardware and software
    d. Technology support tools

22. Internet locations identified with a Uniform Resource Locator (URL) are called
    a. e-mails.
    b. software.
    c. hypermedia.
    d. Web sites.

23. You can find just about anything you want to know about any movie ever made by typing "us.imdb.com" into the site window on your Web browser. The information "us.imdb.com" is best described as a(n)
    a. Web link.
    b. URL.
    c. e-mail address.
    d. home page.

24. Which of the following best describes a URL?
    a. It's a database.
    b. It's a home page.
    c. It's a Web page address.
    d. It's a Web site.

25. "Programs written in a computer language" best describes which of the following?
    a. Drill-and-practice programs
    b. Tutorials
    c. Simulations
    d. Software
    e.

26. Of the following what is most important if technology is to be used effectively to increase learning?
    a. Educators must be clear about the goals they expect to reach when using technology.
    b. Educators must be certain that they are using up-to-date technology, so students don't encounter inconsistencies between the technology they use in school and the technology they use outside school.
    c. Educators must be certain that their technology includes more than computers.
    d. Educators must be certain that their use of technology includes access to the Internet.

27. Of the following what is the best reason for using technology in classrooms?
    a. Technology is now everywhere, so schools need to keep up with the rest of the world.
    b. There is an ever-increasing trend toward using technology, so schools need to be consistent with the trend.
    c. School leaders are advocating the use of technology in teachers' classrooms, so teachers need to be consistent with leaders' goals.
    d. Technology can increase learner motivation, so it can be used as a means of increasing student engagement.

28. For which of the following areas does technology appear *least* promising for promoting learning?
    a. Drill and practice on basic skills
    b. Developing tolerance for dissenting opinions
    c. Developing problem-solving skills
    d. Representing difficult-to-teach topics

29. Assistive technology is designed to
    a. provide alternative mechanisms for students with different learning styles.
    b. increase the rate at which information is provided to students.
    c. provide Internet linkages for students with exceptionalities.
    d. adapt existing technologies (such as computer keyboards) for work with special populations.

30. Communication devices that serve as electronic message centers for a given topic are called
    a. Web sites.
    b. chat rooms.
    c. bulletin boards.
    d. URLs.

31. Research suggests that technology can be most useful in providing practice with quality feedback for what type of student?
    a. Accelerated students
    b. Low-achieving students
    c. Beginning readers
    d. Average learners

32. Which of the following is the best description of computer literacy?
    a. The ability to use computers to access information from the Internet
    b. Being able to use computers to acquire new skills (such as using a tutorial)
    c. Understanding the basic operations and capabilities of computers
    d. Being able to use computers as a communication device (such as using e-mail)

33. Which of the following best describes the primary way that young people use computers in their homes?
    a. To send e-mails
    b. To order goods (such as books and CDs) online
    c. To play computer games
    d. To work on educationally related projects

34. Which of the following is the most accurate description of technology utilization?
    a. Ethnic minorities use computers more frequently than nonminorities at school but less frequently at home.
    b. Household income clearly predicts computer use at home but less clearly predicts computer use at school.
    c. Schools with more disadvantaged students have fewer computers but better access to the Internet.
    d. Females use computers less than do males at the high school level, but the gap narrows in college.

35. Which of the following best describes the relationship between household income and the use of computers in people's homes?
    a. Children of high-income parents (parents who make more than $75,000 per year) have nearly four times the access to computers in homes as do children of low-income parents (parents who make $20,000 or less per year).
    b. Children of high-income parents have a slightly greater access to computers (about 15% greater) than do children of low-income parents.
    c. No relationship exists between access to computers in the home and parental income.
    d. Children of low-income parents have a slightly greater access to computers in the home than do children of high-income parents because low-income parents see computers as a way to help their children catch up.

36. Which of the following best describes boys' and girls' tendencies to be involved in technology enrichment experiences (such as enrolling in computer clubs or taking summer computer classes)?
   a. Boys' and girls' tendencies to be involved in technology enrichment experiences are about equal.
   b. Girls are slightly more likely (about 10% more likely) than boys to be involved in technology enrichment experiences.
   c. Boys are slightly more likely (about 10% more likely) than girls to be involved in technology enrichment experiences.
   d. Boys are much more likely (about three times more likely) than girls to be involved in technology enrichment experience.

Items for Analysis and Critical Thinking

37. Which of the following best illustrates the use of technology to support instruction?
   a. An elementary teacher has his students work on a drill-and-practice program to help them learn their math facts until they become automatic. A Spanish teacher provides her students with a tutorial to help them acquire Spanish vocabulary.
   b. A science teacher has his students practice the symbols of the elements on the periodic table using a computer software program.
   c. A science teacher has her students work on a computer simulation that gives them data about the melting points of a variety of solids.

38. Which of the following best illustrates the use of technology to deliver instruction?
   a. A math teacher has her students complete a tutorial that helps them learn to solve simple algebraic equations.
   b. A science teacher has her students complete a simulation on the dissection of a shark.
   c. An English teacher shows his students a videotape of *The Scarlet Letter*.
   d. A social studies teacher shows his students a DVD of different aspects of the geography of Asia.

39. Henry Jackson is working on problems, such as 6 x 9 =. When he types 48 as an answer, this appears on the screen: "Henry, you're not thinking as clearly as you're capable of. Try once more." He then types 54, and "Dynamite, Henry!! Now we're getting somewhere" appears on the screen. Which of the following best describes the use of technology in this case?
   a. Henry was using a database from which the specific examples were drawn.
   b. Henry was using a drill-and-practice program to help him learn his math facts.
   c. Henry was using a tutorial to help him understand specific information about math.
   d. Henry was involved in a problem-solving activity that helped him understand math.

40. A teacher uses a brief clip on a videotape that shows a falling ball in slow motion to illustrate the acceleration of a freely falling object. Which of the following best describes the way the teacher is using technology in this case?
   a. The video clip is a form of assistive technology since it assists the teacher in her presentation.
   b. The video clip is a technology tool because it is used to make the teacher's presentation clearer.
   c. The video clip is used to support the teacher's instruction because illustrating acceleration would have been difficult in any other way.
   d. The video clip helps the teacher assess the students' understanding based on their comments and questions about what they have seen.

41. A French teacher wants her students to increase their knowledge of basic French terms. Which of the following would be the most effective use of technology to help her reach her goal?
   a. A simulation
   b. A tutorial
   c. A spreadsheet
   d. A drill-and-practice program

42. A pre-algebra teacher wants his students to be able to simplify expressions, such as 8 + 6(5 -3)/4 - 7. Of the following which would be the most effective use of technology to help him reach his goal?
   a. A simulation
   b. A drill-and-practice program
   c. A database
   d. A tutorial

43. Some computer software allows you to conduct a virtual frog dissection to see the organs and other body parts of the frog without cutting up an actual frog. Which of the following most accurately describes this use of technology?
   a. You are using a simulation to examine the parts of a frog.
   b. You are using a database to gather information about a frog.
   c. You are using a tutorial to understand the organs and other body parts of a frog.
   d. You are using hypermedia to understand the frog dissection.

44. A teacher has her students read a section of their textbook on the westward expansion of the United States in the nineteenth century, complete a simulation on difficulties pioneers faced as they moved westward, and watch a DVD of a re-creation of an actual westward trek. Which of the following best describes the teacher's efforts?
   a. The use of software
   b. The use of hardware
   c. The use of tutorials
   d. The use of hypermedia

45. You've typed a comment in an e-mail message that is read by everyone who is online at the time. This type of electronic mail communication is best described as a(n)
   a. e-mail message.
   b. bulletin board discussion.
   c. URL message.
   d. chatroom discussion.

46. Four teachers are at a party and are discussing reasons for using technology in their respective classrooms. Tracy comments, "My principal loves it. In fact, he commented in a faculty meeting about how pleased he was that we're putting our kids on computers."
   Ryan responds, "Yes, and we've got the kids on the 'Net now. A lot of them are spending quite a bit of time 'surfing.'"
   Kevin adds, "Yeah, and we've got more computers in our school than any other school in the district has."
   "Sure," Jim nods, "and I've got two slower kids who are just about up with the rest of the class on their math facts now, since they've been using the computer."
   The teacher who has the best reason for utilizing technology is
   a. Tracy.
   b. Ryan.
   c. Kevin.
   d. Jim.

47. A university in your area is offering a class in Chinese to interested people in rural areas in your state by connecting the people to the university with technology. Which of the following best describes this program?
   a. The Internet
   b. Distance education
   c. E-mail
   d. Hypermedia

48. You want your students to determine how the natural resources a country possesses affect the country's economy. The students go to the library and the Internet to gather information about the types of resources that exist in a variety of countries, such as Argentina, the United States, Russia, Canada, Japan, Nigeria, and India. They also gather information about the economies of these countries, and with your guidance they put the information into a database. Then, again with your guidance, they summarize the information about each country and report to the class, and you conduct a whole-class discussion in an effort to make generalizations about the relationships between natural resources and economies. Of the following which best describes your teaching strategy?
   a. You were using a hypermedia strategy since the students were using both print and electronic materials as resources.
   b. You were using a tutorial strategy since you guided students throughout the learning activity.
   c. You were using a problem-based learning strategy since you presented the students with a problem, and they had to gather information to solve it.
   d. You were using a Web-based strategy since students used the Internet as a primary source of information for the project.

Extended-Response Items

49. The quality of existing educational software varies greatly for two primary reasons. Identify and explain the two reasons. (4 points)

50. Describe three important assessment functions that can be supported by computers, and give an example of each. (6 points)

51. Identify two advantages and two disadvantages of Internet communication, and explain each. (8 points)

52. The issue of access to technology in schools isn't clear. Describe and explain the two sides of the access issue. (4 points)

53. Identify and explain the advantages and disadvantages of placing computers in classrooms as compared to putting them in computer labs. (4 points)

54. The issue of what information students should have a right to access on the Internet has become contentious. Describe and explain both sides of the issue. (4 points)

55. Curricular match with instructional goals, curricular pressures, and preparation-time constraints are instructional issues in the use of technology in schools. Explain each. (6 points)

CHAPTER THIRTEEN

DEVELOPING AS A PROFESSIONAL

Knowledge-Level Items

1. In the United States which of the following best describes the number of men in teaching compared to that of women?
   a. Men and women each make up about half the teaching force.
   b. Women make up slightly more than half the teaching force.
   c. Women make up more than three fourths of the teaching force.
   d. Women make up more than 90 percent of the teaching force.

2. Consider the percentage of cultural minorities, such as African Americans or Hispanics, in the teaching population. Which of the following statements is most accurate?
   a. Slightly more than 10 percent of the teaching force is made up of cultural minorities, but the percentage is increasing rapidly (about a 10% increase per year).
   b. Slightly more than 10 percent of the teaching force is made up of cultural minorities, and the percentage is increasing slightly (about a 2% increase per year).
   c. Slightly more than 10 percent of the teaching force is made up of cultural minorities, and the percentage has remained constant for the last 10 years.
   d. Slightly more than 10 percent of the teaching force is made up of cultural minorities, but the percentage has decreased slightly over the last 10 years.

3. Which of the following statements most accurately describes the population of students in today's schools who are members of cultural minorities?
   a. Nearly a third of school-aged children in the United States are members of cultural minorities, and the percentage of the total school population is about the same as it has been for the last 10 years.
   b. Nearly a third of school-aged children in the United States are members of cultural minorities, and the percentage is rapidly increasing.
   c. Nearly half of school-aged children in the United States are members of cultural minorities, but the percentage of the total school population is decreasing slightly.
   d. Nearly half of school-aged children in the United States are members of cultural minorities, and the percentage is rapidly increasing.

4. Which of the following statements best describes teachers now entering the teaching force as compared to existing teachers?
   a. Teachers now entering the workforce are more likely to be male, younger, and a member of a cultural minority than those presently teaching.
   b. Teachers now entering the workforce are more likely to be female, older, and a member of a cultural minority than those presently teaching.
   c. Teachers now entering the workforce are more likely to be male, younger, and white than those presently teaching.
   d. Teachers now entering the workforce are more likely to be female, younger, and white than those presently teaching.

5. Which of the following statements best compares the percentage of new teachers who leave the profession after their first year and the overall percentage of those who leave each year?
   a. Beginning teachers leave the profession at more than twice the rate of teachers overall (about 15% compared to 6%).
   b. Beginning teachers leave the profession at a slightly higher rate than teachers overall (about 8% compared to 6%).
   c. Beginning teachers leave the profession at almost exactly the same rate as teachers overall.
   d. Beginning teachers leave the profession at a slightly lower rate than teachers overall (about 4% compared to 6%).

6. Experienced teachers who provide guidance and support for beginning teachers are most commonly called
   a. supervisors.
   b. support staff.
   c. mentors.
   d. peer teachers.

7. Which of the following best describes the influence of mentoring programs on the rate at which beginning teachers leave the profession after one year?
   a. Mentoring programs have little effect on whether or not teachers leave the profession after one year.
   b. Beginning teachers involved in mentoring programs are slightly *more* likely than those not involved in mentoring programs to leave the profession after one year.
   c. Beginning teachers involved in mentoring programs are slightly *less* likely than those not involved in mentoring programs to leave the profession after one year (about 10% less).
   d. Beginning teachers involved in mentoring programs are less than half as likely as those not involved in mentoring programs to leave the profession after one year.

8. Which of the following statements best describes beginning teachers' beliefs about their teaching ability?
   a. Beginning teachers are uncertain about their teaching ability when they begin, but they are more self-assured by the end of their first year.
   b. Beginning teachers are confident about their teaching ability when they begin, but their confidence decreases when they encounter the realities of classroom life.
   c. Beginning teachers are uncertain about their teaching ability when they begin, and their uncertainty remains until about their third year of experience.
   d. Beginning teachers are confident about their teaching ability when they begin, and their confidence remains high at the end of their first year.

9. Which of the following statements best describes beginning teachers' expectations about their abilities to help children learn?
   a. Beginning teachers expect their confidence in their abilities to help children learn to *increase* as they gather experience.
   b. Beginning teachers expect their confidence in their abilities to help children learn to *decrease* as they gather experience.
   c. Beginning teachers expect their confidence in their abilities to help children learn to remain high and steady as they gather experience.
   d. Beginning teachers expect their confidence in their abilities to help children learn to *decrease* during the first few months but then to *increase* as they settle into their jobs.

10. Which of the following statements best describes beginning teachers' beliefs about how they will learn to be effective teachers?
    a. Beginning teachers believe that they will learn most of what they need to know about becoming an effective teacher in their university classes.
    b. Beginning teachers believe that they will learn most of what they need to know about becoming an effective teacher in their university classes combined with pre-internships.
    c. Beginning teachers believe that they will learn most of what they need to know about becoming an effective teacher when they get into full-time experiences in classrooms.
    d. Beginning teachers believe that they will learn most of what they need to know about becoming an effective teacher in their university classes combined with their internships (student teaching experiences).

11. Of the following which is the most accurate description of beginning teachers' beliefs about what makes a teacher effective?
    a. The most effective teachers are those who are able to establish close relationships with their students.
    b. The most effective teachers are those who genuinely care about their students.
    c. The most effective teachers are those who are enthusiastic about the topics they teach.
    d. The most effective teachers are those able to most clearly explain the content they teach to their students.

12. People who are knowledgeable and highly skilled in a field are most commonly described as
    a. master teachers.
    b. experts.
    c. technicians.
    d. professionals.

13. Which of the following statements best describes the importance of knowledge of content (such as knowledge of history) in being an effective teacher?
    a. If teachers understand content well enough, they will be able to figure out how to teach it effectively.
    b. Knowledge of content is one of the essential kinds of knowledge that effective teachers possess.
    c. Knowledge of content is valuable but not essential for being an effective teacher.
    d. Knowledge of content isn't necessary for becoming an effective teacher; expert teachers learn the content they want to teach when they prepare their lessons.

14. An "understanding of ways of representing content so that it's comprehensible to others" best describes
    a. pedagogical content knowledge.
    b. knowledge of content.
    c. general pedagogical knowledge.
    d. knowledge of learners and learning.

15. Of the following, teacher questioning most closely relates to
    a. pedagogical content knowledge.
    b. knowledge of content.
    c. knowledge of learners and learning.
    d. general pedagogical knowledge.

16. An understanding of instruction and management that transcends individual topics or subject matter areas is best described as
    a. pedagogical content knowledge.
    b. expert knowledge.
    c. general pedagogical knowledge.
    d. knowledge of learning and teaching.

17. The "process by which a state evaluated the credentials of prospective teachers to ensure that they meet the state's professional standards" is best described as
    a. teacher tenure.
    b. teacher licensure.
    c. general pedagogical assessment.
    d. National Board certification.

18. Which of the following are requirements for teacher licensure in most of our country's states?
    (1) Completing a bachelor's degree including a general education component
    (2) Passing a test of basic reading, writing, and math skills
    (3) Passing a test measuring background in a subject-matter area (such as history)
    (4) Passing a test measuring understanding of learning and teaching

    a. 1, 2, 3, 4
    b. 1, 2, 3
    c. 1, 3
    d. 1, 3, 4

19. Which of the following best describes the attrition rate of people who go through alternative licensure programs as compared to those who go through traditional licensure programs?
   a. The attrition rate of people who go through alternative and traditional licensure programs is approximately the same (about 30% after 2 years).
   b. The attrition rate of people who go through alternative licensure programs is slightly lower than the attrition rate for people going through traditional licensure programs (about 25% compared to 30% after 2 years).
   c. The attrition rate of people who go through alternative licensure programs is slightly higher than the attrition rate for people going through traditional licensure programs (about 30% compared to 25% after 2 years).
   d. The attrition rate of people who go through alternative licensure programs is nearly three times greater than the attrition rate for people going through traditional licensure programs.

20. "Special recognition by a professional organization indicating that an individual has met certain requirements specified by the organization" best describes which of the following?
   a. Teacher licensure
   b. Teacher certification
   c. Teacher tenure
   d. Teacher professionalism

21. Which of the following best describes the goals of the National Board for Professional Teaching Standards?
   a. To strengthen teaching as a profession and improve the quality of education
   b. To increase teachers' knowledge of content and understanding of strategies needed to deliver the content
   c. To improve the quality of alternative licensure programs and reduce the attrition rate of new teachers
   d. To increase teacher salaries and improve teachers' working conditions

22. Which of the following statements best describes the relationship between the propositions of the National Board for Professional Teaching Standards (NBPTS) and the four types of knowledge—knowledge of content, pedagogical content knowledge, general pedagogical knowledge, and knowledge of learners and learning—that research indicates effective teachers possess?
   a. The NBPTS propositions place strong emphasis on knowledge of content and less emphasis on the other forms of knowledge.
   b. The NBPTS propositions place strong—and approximately equal—emphasis on each of the four types of knowledge that research indicates effective teachers possess.
   c. The NBPTS propositions place primary emphasis on learner motivation and learner diversity.
   d. The NBPTS propositions place primary emphasis on the importance of self-esteem in learners' overall development.

23. Which of the following best describes the primary purpose for creating a professional portfolio?
   a. To collect work products (such as written papers and videotapes of teaching experiences) during the course of a teacher-preparation program
   b. To gather experiences that extend beyond paper-and-pencil tests
   c. To document the knowledge and skills of a prospective teacher
   d. To help clarify the teaching goals of a prospective teacher

24. A document that provides an overview of a prospective teacher's background and experience best describes which of the following?
   a. A professional portfolio
   b. A professional résumé
   c. A professional certification
   d. Professional tenure

25. With respect to instructors' opinions, which of the following is the most important reason for students to attend all classes and be on time?
    a. Instructors view missing classes as unprofessional behavior by students.
    b. Instructors worry that the students will miss some important content if they miss classes.
    c. Instructors take it as a personal reflection on their teaching if students miss classes.
    d. Missing classes is disruptive to instructors' routines.

26. For which of the following are job opportunities likely to be the greatest?
    a. Secondary social studies
    b. Middle school English
    c. High school biology
    d. Middle school math

27. For which of the following are job opportunities likely to be the greatest?
    a. Teaching math in a suburban school
    b. Teaching chemistry in an inner-city school
    c. Teaching physics in a suburban school
    d. Teaching Spanish in a suburban school

28. Consider the relationship between the use of standard English and interviewing effectively. Which of the following is the most accurate statement?
    a. You should be yourself and use the language and grammar that is natural for you; interviewers react most positively to a candidate that is genuine.
    b. Interviewers realize that candidates' grammar and language vary, so they don't assess candidates on the basis of the grammar they use.
    c. Interviewers are forbidden from using a candidate's language, grammar, or dialect in assessing a candidate's qualifications for a job.
    d. You should use standard English and grammar because a candidate's use of language creates an impression of the candidate's professional ability.

29. A collection of important documents you'll need to submit when you apply for a teaching position is best described as a
    a. portfolio.
    b. résumé.
    c. credentials file.
    d. license.

30. A document that provides an overview of your background and experience is called a
    a. portfolio.
    b. résumé.
    c. credentials file.
    d. license.

31. Professional experiences for beginning teachers that help ease their transition into teaching are most commonly called
    a. induction programs.
    b. alternative licensure.
    c. certification.
    d. mentoring experiences.

32. Which of the following is the best description of formative evaluation?
    a. The process of providing professional experiences for beginning teachers that help them make the transition to classroom work
    b. The process of gathering materials—such as lesson plans, worksheets, and videotaped lessons—that are used to represent a teacher's work
    c. The process of gathering information about teachers' competence and making administrative decisions about retention and promotion
    d. The process of gathering information and providing feedback that teachers can use to improve their instruction

33. The process of gathering information about teachers' competence and making administrative decisions about retention and promotion is called
    a. formative evaluation.
    b. mentoring.
    c. certification.
    d. summative evaluation.

34. The process of identifying a specific, school-related question and gathering information to try to answer it is best described as
    a. action research.
    b. alternative certification.
    c. formative evaluation.
    d. summative evaluation.

35. Which of the following best describes the concept certification?
    a. Information about teachers' competence that is gathered for the purpose of making administrative decisions about retention and promotion
    b. The process states use to ensure that teachers meet professional standards
    c. Recognition by a professional organization that an individual has met requirements specified by the organization
    d. The process of gathering information and providing feedback that teachers can use to improve their instruction

Items for Analysis and Critical Thinking

Use the following information for Items 36–39:

Tim Thrift, a world history teacher, wants his students to understand the characteristics of New Stone Age people, so he prepares the following vignette.
> You're part of an archeological team, and you've discovered artifacts at a site. Some of the artifacts include spear points that are still quite sharp, having been ground precisely from hard stone. You also see several cattle and sheep skulls and some threads that appear to be the remains of coarsely woven fabric.

Tim has his vignette printed in large type on an overhead that he has ready and waiting. As part of his classroom routines he has trained his students to be in their seats and waiting quietly when the bell rings.

36. Which of the following best describes the knowledge Tim demonstrated in preparing his vignette?
    a. He demonstrated thorough knowledge of content.
    b. He demonstrated both knowledge of content and pedagogical content knowledge.
    c. He demonstrated knowledge of content and knowledge of learners and learning.
    d. He demonstrated knowledge of content and general pedagogical knowledge.

37. Tim prepared his vignette because he believed that the description of New Stone Age people as presented in his students' textbooks was too abstract to be meaningful. Of the following which best describes the type of knowledge on which Tim's belief was primarily based?
   a.   His knowledge of content
   b.   His pedagogical content knowledge
   c.   His knowledge of learners and learning
   d.   His general pedagogical knowledge

38. Having his vignette ready on an overhead and having trained his students to be in their seats and waiting quietly when the bell rings best demonstrate what kind of knowledge?
   a.   His knowledge of content
   b.   Both his knowledge of content and his pedagogical content knowledge
   c.   His general pedagogical knowledge
   d.   His knowledge of learners and learning

39. Which of the following statements best describes Tim's expertise?
   a.   The evidence indicates that Tim is an expert teacher because he demonstrated each of the four kinds of knowledge—knowledge of content, pedagogical content knowledge, general pedagogical knowledge, and knowledge of learners and learning—necessary to be an effective teacher.
   b.   The evidence indicates that Tim is an expert teacher because he demonstrated thorough knowledge of content, which is the most important form of knowledge for expert teachers.
   c.   The evidence indicates that Tim is an expert teacher because his students were very orderly, and classroom management is teachers' number one concern.
   d.   The evidence indicates that Tim is a novice teacher because he didn't do a hands-on activity with his students, and hands-on activities are most effective for promoting student learning.

40. Which of the following statements best describes the following quote: "The teacher understands and uses a variety of instructional strategies to encourage students' development of critical thinking, problem solving, and performance skills"?
   a.   It is a description of one of the propositions of the National Board for Professional Teaching Standards, which describes certification for advanced professionals.
   b.   It is a description of one of the principles of the Interstate New Teacher Assessment and Support Consortium (INTASC), which describes what advanced professionals (veteran teachers) should know and be able to do.
   c.   It is a description of one of the principles of the Interstate New Teacher Assessment and Support Consortium (INTASC), which describes what beginning teachers should know and be able to do.
   d.   It is a statement from a teachers' code of ethics, which describes their ethical responsibilities in working with students of all ability levels.

Use the following vignette for Items 41–43:

Jason, Christie, Damon, and Carol are walking across the campus as they head toward one of their teacher-preparation courses. "Where are you going?" Jason asks Damon, as Damon turns off and heads away from the other three.

"I'm not going today," Damon shrugs. "I don't see how this stuff is going to help me be a better teacher, and I don't think Wilburn [the professor in the course] will miss me anyway. I asked Wilburn how this stuff was relevant, but he didn't seem to have that great an answer."

"What about your homework?" Carol asks.

"I didn't finish it," Damon continued. "I'll slip it under his door. He doesn't count off for late work anyway."

Just as class is beginning, Carol asks, "Dr. Wilburn? You said last time that Progessivism essentially disappeared by the mid-twentieth century, but awhile back we learned that hands-on activities are one characteristic of Progressivism, and most of our other instructors emphasize hands-on activities. Those two ideas don't seem to be consistent."

"That's an excellent observation, Carol," Dr. Wilburn nods. "What does anyone else think about her comment?"

"How do you think Wilburn liked your comment?" Jason asks Carol after class.

"I don't think he minded," she replied. "He actually seemed to like it. By the way, why don't you two speak up," Carol queries, looking at both Jason and Christie. "You both get better grades on the tests than I do."

"*B* pluses instead of *B*s," Christie waves. "Big deal. I go in and see Wilburn quite a bit. I like to tell him what a great teacher he is. He just smiles when I say it."

"You got an *A* didn't you?" Carol asks Jason.

"Yeah," Jason smiles. "I studied my butt off for the test because I had missed a couple classes earlier in the semester."

"I never miss class," Carol nods. "I always feel a little lost about what's going on if I'm not there."

41. The student most likely to develop the *best* professional reputation is likely to be
    a.   Jason because he gets the best grades of the four students.
    b.   Christie because she seems to have the best personal relationship with Dr. Wilburn.
    c.   Damon because he thinks the most critically about the worth of the class.
    d.   Carol because she is the most conscientious and involved in the class.

42. The student who is *least* likely to develop a positive professional reputation is
    a.   Jason because he's missed a couple classes.
    b.   Christie because she is trying to "suck up" to Dr. Wilburn.
    c.   Damon because he's the least interested in learning for its own sake.
    d.   Carol because she asks questions that seem critical of the course content.

43. Of the following what is Dr. Wilburn's most likely reaction to Christie telling him what a great teacher he is?
    a.   He will take the comments at face value; flattery is difficult to see through.
    b.   He will react very positively and view Christie very positively as a student.
    c.   He will react negatively to Christie repeatedly coming in for help, but he will react positively to the compliment.
    d.   He is likely to react positively to Christie asking for help, but he will be skeptical of her repeated compliments.

44. You have job offers at two different schools, and you're trying to decide which one to accept. Of the following which is the most important factor to consider in making your decision?
    a.   The commitment and leadership of the school principal because the principal sets the tone for the school climate and working conditions
    b.   The attitude of the teachers in the rooms next to you because they're the people with whom you'll most interact
    c.   The amount of technology you have available in the school because it indicates the amount of instructional support you'll receive
    d.   Your salary because it will determine how satisfied you are on the job

45. Of the following which is likely to be most important for you in surviving your first year of teaching?
    a.   Your ability to use sophisticated forms of instruction, such as guided discovery, because they strongly influence student motivation
    b.   Your ability to do group work and cooperative learning because they are powerful strategies for getting students involved
    c.   Your communication with your colleagues because they will be able to give you helpful survival tips
    d.   Your organizational skills because they will save you time, and lack of time is an important problem for first-year teachers

46. With respect to surviving your first year of teaching, which of the following statements best describes the relationship between classroom management and effective instruction?
   a. Classroom management is a prerequisite to effective instruction; order must first be established before teachers can instruct effectively.
   b. Orderly classrooms are a result or an outcome of effective instruction; if instruction is effective, classroom management takes care of itself.
   c. Classroom management and effective instruction are interdependent; it is virtually impossible to effectively teach in a chaotic classroom, and orderly classrooms are virtually impossible if instruction is ineffective.
   d. Classroom management and effective instruction are not related; classroom management refers to students' behaviors, and effective instruction refers to teachers' behaviors.

47. Which of the following are helpful suggestions for preventing classroom management problems in your first year of teaching?
   (1) Plan procedures (such as how students will turn in papers) in advance.
   (2) Learn students' names.
   (3) Use as much cooperative learning as possible.
   (4) Practice questioning skills.

   a. 1, 2, 3, 4
   b. 1, 2, 4
   c. 1, 3
   d. 2, 3, 4

Extended-Response Items

48. Identify and explain three commonly cited reasons that beginning teachers give for leaving the profession after their first year. (6 points)

49. Describe the beliefs of beginning teachers with respect to effective instruction, that is, what beginning teachers believe effective teachers do when they want to help students understand a particular topic. Explain why they are likely to have this belief. (4 points)

50. Alternative licensure has become an important topic in the preparation of teachers. Explain the arguments supporting and criticizing alternative licensure. (4 points)

51. Describe the steps involved in creating a professional portfolio, and then include a specific example of each step. (10 points)

52. Identify one advantage and one disadvantage of electronic portfolios as compared to traditional portfolios. Explain each. (4 points)

53. Describe and explain four ways to make yourself marketable for your first job. (8 points)

54. Describe action research. Then identify and illustrate four steps that teachers should take in planning and conducting action-research activities. (10 points)

CHAPTER ONE ANSWERS

1.	d	11.	a	21.	b	31.	d
2.	b	12.	c	22.	c	32.	b
3.	b	13.	c	23.	d	33.	b
4.	b	14.	b	24.	a	34.	b
5.	c	15.	c	25.	d	35.	d
6.	d	16.	b	26.	a	36.	a
7.	a	17.	c	27.	d	37.	b
8.	c	18.	c	28.	c	38.	d
9.	d	19.	a	29.	d	39.	b
10.	b	20.	d	30.	a	40.	c

41. b   The ability to represent topics in ways that are understandable to students illustrates pedagogical content knowledge.

42. d   Kominko is analytical and self-critical about her work. ("I don't think I went through enough examples . . . I'm going to reteach it next week, and I'm going to do it differently.") These are characteristics of reflection.

43. b   Juanita demonstrated a desire to acquire a specialized body of knowledge, and a specialized body of knowledge is one characteristic of a profession. She also demonstrated the autonomy characteristic of a professional.

44. c   David's comment "I'd rather have someone tell me how to get them to behave" is more characteristic of a technician than a professional.

45. b   Intentionally embarrassing a student is in direct violation of teachers' professional code of ethics.

46. d   Manuel is involved in decision making. He recognizes that "they think that adjectives are words that go just before nouns," and he attempts to solve that problem in an effort to reach his goal of helping the students have a clear concept of adjectives.

47. c   Denial of graduation from high school is characteristic of a high-stakes test.

48. b   Making teachers responsible for student performance on tests illustrates accountability.

49. d   A prospective teacher's collection of work is called a portfolio.

50. Criteria for response:
The response should include the desire to contribute to the world and to work with young people. People who choose teaching typically have strong desires to make the world a better place, and teacher salaries typically aren't high enough to motivate people to choose teaching based on monetary rewards.

51. Criteria for response:
The response should address intrinsic rewards, such as emotional rewards and intellectual rewards, as well as extrinsic rewards, such as favorable working conditions and desirable vacations. The response should then include a specific example of each (such as a former student coming back for a visit as an example of an emotional reward).

52. Criteria for response:
The response should include some of the following: unresponsive parents, demanding administrators who are not supportive, colleagues who are difficult to get along with, and unmotivated and disruptive students. The response should include an example of each (such as parents who won't return phone calls as an example of unresponsive parents).

53. Criteria for response:
The response should include a specialized body of knowledge, extended training for licensure, autonomy, and ethical standards of conduct. The response should then include an example of each (such as teachers being required to complete an undergraduate degree and pass an exam to be licensed).

54. Criteria for response:
The response should identify knowledge of content, pedagogical content knowledge, general pedagogical knowledge, and knowledge of learners and learning as the four kinds of knowledge. The response should then include an example of each (such as having a thorough grasp of American history as an example of knowledge of content).

55. Criteria for response:

The response should address training, unique function, autonomy, and accountability. An argument against teaching being a profession would suggest that teachers aren't well trained, and they lack a unique function, autonomy, and accountability. An argument for teaching being a profession would suggest the opposite. Then the response should include information that illustrates the position (such as arguing that teachers lack a unique function since many other people including parents and the clergy "teach" or that people other than doctors practice medicine).

56. Criteria for response:

The response should include the question of whether the tests are accurate enough to direct decisions about students' academic lives; the question of technical problems with the tests; the suggestion that the test score differences between minority and nonminority students reflect culture and language differences rather than actual differences in achievement; and/or the question of whether basing promotion or graduation on one test score is valid.

CHAPTER TWO ANSWERS

1.	a	11.	d	21.	c	31.	a
2.	a	12.	d	22.	b	32.	b
3.	d	13.	b	23.	d	33.	d
4.	a	14.	c	24.	a	34.	d
5.	b	15.	a	25.	c	35.	d
6.	c	16.	d	26.	b	36.	d
7.	b	17.	c	27.	b	37.	c
8.	b	18.	b	28.	a	38.	c
9.	a	19.	d	29.	c		
10.	d	20.	a	30.	b		

39. a The combination of a reading group in progress, students working on a seatwork assignment, and an intercom announcement illustrates the multidimensional aspects of teaching.

40. b Juan felt he needed to intervene immediately to prevent a minor disruption from escalating into a major one.

41. d Several events happening at the same time illustrates the simultaneous aspect of teaching.

42. c Several of the students looking up is evidence that teaching is a public activity. Someone observes virtually everything that teachers do.

43. a Withitness indicates that a teacher knows what's going on in all parts of the classroom all the time. Juan seeing Bill tap Louanne the first time he did it is an indicator that Juan knew what was going on in his classroom.

44. d The ability to conduct, or attend to, two events at the same time is evidence of overlapping.

45. c Holding students to high standards and not accepting sloppy or thoughtless work is an indicator of respect.

46. a Having crackers to feed hungry children is an indicator of caring.

47. d Meeting with other teachers to discuss professional issues is evidence of being a collaborative colleague.

48. b Being organized for the day allowed Susan to maximize her time for instruction, which is evidence of being able to create a productive learning environment.

49. c When Susan sent information home, she was communicating with parents, which is part of being an ambassador to the public.

50. e Wanting to learn, in any form, is evidence of being a learner and a reflective practitioner.

51. Criteria for response:
The response should indicate that Japanese teachers spend only about half as much time directly involved in instruction as do American teachers. The response should suggest that Japanese teachers have more autonomy and more decision-making power, so they are treated more professionally than are American teachers.

52. Criteria for response:
The response should refer to and explain the four-by-four block schedule and the alternating-day block schedule. The response should also include suggested advantages, such as less time spent in transitions from one class to another.

53. Criteria for response:
The response should include four of the following dimensions—multidimensional, simultaneous, immediate, unpredictable, or public. The response should then include examples (such as a teacher conducting a reading group at the same time other students are doing seatwork, an example of the simultaneous dimension).

54. Criteria for response:
The response should include four of the following: caring professional, creator of productive learning environments, ambassador to the public, collaborative colleague, and learner and reflective practitioner. The response should then include examples (such as a teacher making phone calls to parents on his or her own time after school, an example of the caring professional role).

55. Criteria for response:
The response should state that the teaching force is about three fourths female, nearly 90 percent white, and of an average age in the early 40s.

56. Criteria for response:

The response should state that people now entering the teaching force are younger, more likely to be female, and less likely to be a cultural minority than in the past.

57. Criteria for response:

The response should include the need for minority role models, effective instruction for cultural minorities, and the ability to bring different perspectives to learning activities. The response should explain each (e.g., that minority students who see a minority teacher succeed are more likely to believe that they can succeed than if they see a successful white teacher).

1.	a	12.	b	23.	a	34.	d
2.	b	13.	b	24.	d	35.	c
3.	d	14.	c	25.	a	36.	b
4.	d	15.	d	26.	a	37.	a
5.	c	16.	b	27.	a	38.	d
6.	a	17.	b	28.	d	39.	a
7.	a	18.	c	29.	c	40.	c
8.	b	19.	b	30.	a	41.	a
9.	a	20.	b	31.	c	42.	b
10.	d	21.	b	32.	d	43.	c
11.	c	22.	d	33.	d	44.	a

45. b   African American students' communication patterns can be different from those of white Americans, making African American students more likely to misinterpret a statement that doesn't directly say, "Put your papers away now."

46. c   Some evidence indicates that the communication patterns of Native Americans are slower paced and even deferential, compared to the communication of white Americans. This can result in a student like Michael being less comfortable in a quick-paced question-and-answer activity.

47. a   Traditional conceptions of intelligence define it as the ability to solve problems, think in the abstract, and acquire knowledge. Tony appears to have some trouble thinking in the abstract, and he acquires knowledge at a slower rate than do his peers.

48. d   Tony would probably be low in logical-mathematical and linguistic intelligence and high in interpersonal and musical intelligence. We don't have evidence for the others, such as spatial.

49. a   Working quickly and making errors is characteristic of an impulsive learning style.

50. b   Giving a lot of thought before answering is characteristic of a reflective learning style.

51. d   Marisa is demonstrating that she is aware of the way she learns most effectively ("I get it better if I actually write an answer first"), and she controls those factors by actually writing the answers. These are the characteristics of metacognition.

52. Criteria for response:
The response should state that the minority population will increase substantially over the next 20 years but that the non-Hispanic white population will decrease in proportion. The response should also indicate that teachers will need to be better prepared to work with cultural minorities than they have been in the past.

53. Criteria for response:
The response should state that culturally responsive teaching includes accepting and valuing differences, accommodating different cultural learning styles, and building on students' cultural backgrounds. The response should then include examples (such as having students identify their ethnic homelands on a map, an example of accepting and valuing differences).

54. Criteria for response:
The response should include five differences from among the following: Girls enter school even or ahead of boys but leave school behind; girls score lower on the SAT and ACT, especially at the higher achievement levels; and women score lower on all sections of the Graduate Record Exam. Boys outnumber girls in remedial English and math classes, are held back in grades more often, and are two to three times more likely to be placed in special education classes; boys consistently receive lower grades than girls and score lower than girls on both direct and indirect measures of writing skills; boys are more likely to be involved in serious misbehavior; and boys earn fewer bachelor and master's degrees than do women.

55. Criteria for response:
The response should indicate that Gardner's view emphasizes that intelligence is composed of several different traits, whereas traditional views of intelligence are much narrower, essentially limited to linguistic and logical-mathematical intelligence.

56. Criteria for response:
The response should indicate that cultural learning styles primarily represent differences in patterns of interaction between people. It should then include an example (such as Native Americans being uncomfortable in briskly paced question-and-answer activities).

CHAPTER FOUR ANSWERS

1.	a	12.	c	23.	a	34.	d
2.	a	13.	c	24.	d	35.	b
3.	c	14	c	25.	b	36.	d
4.	b	15.	d	26.	b	37.	d
5.	b	16.	a	27.	a	38.	b
6.	d	17.	d	28.	b	39.	a
7.	d	18.	b	29.	c	40.	d
8.	d	19.	d	30.	a	41.	a
9.	b	20.	d	31.	a	42.	b
10.	a	21.	b	32.	b	43.	a
11.	b	22.	d	33.	c		

44. a   Ellen's father demonstrates an authoritarian parenting style, and research indicates that students who become bullies often come from homes where parents are authoritarian, hostile, and rejecting.

45. c   Experts recommend a zero tolerance policy for harassment, particularly for homosexual youth, who are much more likely to use drugs and commit suicide than are students from the general school population.

46. c   The combination of abrupt changes in school performance, becoming withdrawn, and losing interest in appearance are all indicators of depression and potential suicide.

47. c   If suicide is even a remote possibility, students need immediate help, so contacting a school counselor or psychologist is essential.

48. d   Legally teachers are protected from liability in cases of suspected abuse if the report is honestly made and is based on evidence.

49. d   Calvin's parents are divorced; he is low SES, a cultural minority, and male; and he isn't interested in extracurricular activities.

50. a   Ariel comes from an intact family, his English is improving rapidly, and he is involved and successful in extracurricular activities.

51. Criteria for response:

The response should state that about 7 out of 10 women with children are in the workforce, and the divorce rate has quadrupled in the last 20 years. The response should also include the implication for teachers that parents, in general, spend less time with their children than they have spent in the past, and teachers will probably get less parental support than they have gotten in the past.

52. Criteria for response:

The response should include three factors from the following: basic needs, family stability, school-related experience, interaction patterns in the home, and parental attitudes and values. It should then include examples (such as high-SES parents reading and talking to their children, taking them to places like zoos, museums, and art galleries, all to a greater extent than do low-SES parents).

53. Criteria for response:

The response should state that teachers are legally obligated to report suspected cases of child abuse. It should also state that they are protected from liability if the report is honestly made and based on evidence.

54. Criteria for response:

The response should include three criticisms from among the following: Zero tolerance policies don't discriminate between major and minor offenses, offenders are often sent home instead of being retained in school so they're even more likely to get into further trouble, expelled students fall even further behind in their school work, and the policies disproportionately influence cultural minorities. The response should then include examples that explain the criticisms (such as a 6-year-old being suspended for kissing a classmate).

55. Criteria for response:

The response should indicate that student cooperation and motivation will be your primary day-to-day problems. It should also state that the likelihood of violence, while receiving enormous press coverage, is extremely remote.

56. Criteria for response:

The response should include two of the following as characteristics that place him at-risk: He is a male and a cultural minority, and his parents are divorced. It should then include two of the following that suggest that he is not at-risk: He is not low SES, his family structure is positive and supportive, and he is involved and successful in extracurricular activities.

CHAPTER FIVE ANSWERS

1.	a	11.	d	21.	b	31.	c
2.	a	12.	c	22.	c	32.	d
3.	a	13.	a	23.	c	33.	b
4.	c	14.	b	24.	b	34.	c
5.	d	15.	d	25.	b	35.	a
6.	b	16.	d	26.	d	36.	a
7.	d	17.	a	27.	b	37.	b
8.	c	18.	b	28.	c	38.	b
9.	b	19.	a	29.	a	39.	a
10.	c	20.	a	30.	b	40.	d

41. b   Because the southern colonies depended on agriculture, the people tended to live far apart, so creating centralized schools in towns was more difficult than in the middle or northern colonies.

42. a   The middle colonies were the most diverse of the three groups of colonies, and this included religious diversity, which resulted in many of the religious groups creating their own schools.

43. d   The northern colonies were influenced by Puritanism, which assumed that humanity was innately evil.

44. c   The Massachusetts Act of 1647 was intended to create a literate citizenry, which would help combat the forces of evil.

45. b   These philosophers emphasized direct experience, and they historically influenced what is today's learner-centered curriculum and approaches to instruction.

46. b   A common planning period and emphasis in integrating curriculum are characteristics of the middle school philosophy.

47. c   Progressive education emphasizes direct experience (such as hands-on activities). Ashley's students are most involved in direct experiences.

48. Criteria for response:

The response should state that the southern colonies were the most aristocratic, partially because of the practice of slavery and living on large plantations; the middle colonies were the most diverse; and the northern colonies, the most culturally homogeneous with the influence of Puritanism. The response should also include explanations (such as the middle colonies creating parochial schools with different religious orientations because of the religious diversity in those colonies).

49. Criteria for response:

The response should include the following: The colonial period helps us understand why equality in schooling has been difficult to accomplish (because of aristocratic emphasis in the period), why religion and the schools remains an important issue, and how it established a precedent for public support of education. The response should also note that the early national period was significant for the principle of separation of church and state, control of education being moved into the hands of the states, and education being viewed as crucial for the nation's development. Finally, the response should note that the common school movement was significant because the idea of universal, tax-supported education for all was created during this period.

50. Criteria for response:

The response should state that the assimilation movement attempted to bring cultural minorities into the mainstream of American life by emphasizing basic skills and white middle-class values. It should also state that the movement was largely a failure and should include evidence (such as Native Americans going to the boarding schools and then right back to the reservations after leaving the boarding schools).

51. Criteria for response:

The response should state that Booker T. Washington believed that hard work, practical training, and economic cooperation with whites were the keys to success, and W.E.B. Du Bois was committed to changing the status of African Americans and recommended a determined stand against segregation and racism. The response should also address their backgrounds (such as noting that Booker T. Washington was born a slave and was self-taught, whereas W.E.B. Du Bois was born free and educated in integrated schools).

52. Criteria for response:

The response should state that the success of the two programs is mixed. It should also state that some of the programs were poorly designed and implemented, which is the reason for the mixed results.

53. Criteria for response:

The response should include both sides of the issues (such as some minority leaders and women's groups arguing that progress for cultural minorities and women has been too slow and the government should do more, and conservative leaders arguing that civil rights have gone too far and reverse discrimination now exists).

CHAPTER SIX ANSWERS

1.	a	9.	a	17.	c	25.	c
2.	d	10.	b	18.	d	26.	a
3.	d	11	d	19.	d	27.	c
4.	b	12.	c	20.	b	28.	c
5.	c	13.	b	21.	b	29.	b
6.	b	14.	c	22.	b	30.	b
7.	a	15.	a	23.	a	31.	a
8.	c	16.	b	24.	d	32.	a

33. c   When Claire said, "We know that people are motivated by the extent to which they expect to succeed on challenging tasks," she was offering an explanation for motivation, which is based on theory. When she said, "There is information everyone needs in order to function in today's world, and we need to hold kids' feet to the fire to be sure that they learn it," she was talking about the way things *ought to be*, which is philosophy.

34. b   When Antonio said, "I think kids need to learn how to get information on their own. Then they'll be better equipped to function in today's world," he was making a philosophical statement, but his argument didn't include any explanation, so there was no evidence of conclusions based on theory.

35. b   The conclusion was based on records of specific incidents of repair, from which the general conclusion about reliability was made, so this illustrates inductive reasoning.

36. d   These differences are most nearly suggested by epistemology. Epistemology is important for teachers because it suggests the teaching methods that they will use. For example, if teachers believe that the way they come to know what they know results from individual construction of understanding, they will use different methods than they would if they believe that people learn by being told.

37. c   Jennifer concluded "I'm eating too much" based on the major premise "When you take in more calories than you burn, you gain weight" and the minor premise "I've gained 5 pounds in the last 6 months."

38. a   Jennifer's statement "When you take in more calories than you burn, you gain weight" is a proposition from which the rest of her argument follows.

39. b   A minor premise is a fact, and gaining 5 pounds in the last 6 months is, assuming that her readings are accurate, a fact.

40. a   A proposition (major premise) followed by a fact (minor premise) and a conclusion describes deductive reasoning.

41. a   Moral dilemmas are time-honored ideas, and idealists emphasize the importance of ideas being the essence of reality.

42. b   Realism emphasizes that effective schooling prepares students for the world around them by providing them with intellectual tools.

43. c   Problem-based learning and real-world application are educational applications based on pragmatism.

44. c   Karen's approach is based on real-world application—which is a progressivist approach—grounded in pragmatism.

45. d   Emphasis on the contribution of women and cultural minorities is grounded in postmodernism.

46. a   The first teacher believes that Columbus's discovery and opening the New World are essential knowledge that all students should possess.

47. d   Focusing on the exploitation of native people is a theme of postmodernism.

48. Criteria for response:

The response should state that idealism would focus on content that emphasizes time-honored ideas, realism would emphasize content that illustrates natural laws, pragmatism would emphasize curricula and instruction that provide experience with problem solving and the scientific method, and existentialism emphasizes discussion designed to increase individual self-awareness. The response should then include examples (such as a teacher having students read classic literature as an example of an implication of idealism).

49. Criteria for response:

The response should state that both idealism and realism are criticized for being elitist and failing to take feelings and emotions into account, pragmatism is criticized because it places too little value on essential knowledge, and existentialism is criticized for suggesting that people have total freedom. The response should also include explanations (such as pointing out that classic literature is more effective with high achievers than it is with low achievers).

50. Criteria for response:

   The response should state that perennialism is criticized for being elitist, essentialism is criticized for focusing too strongly on basic skills to the exclusion of other parts of the curriculum, progressivism is criticized for too strongly emphasizing the individual and self-esteem at the expense of understanding, and postmodernism is criticized as being too political. The response should also include explanations (such as noting that the postmodernist emphasis on the work of minority authors promotes a political rather than an educational agenda).

51. Criteria for response:

   The response should state that cultural minorities have different approaches to the world, such as Native Americans emphasizing harmony and cooperation because of their history of living in harmony with nature, African Americans valuing feelings and personal relationships, and Asians also valuing harmony and reverence for authority. The response should also include a description of the criticisms of these views (such as the argument that these views are dramatic oversimplifications at best and stereotypes at worst).

52. Criteria for response:

   The response should include information from Table 6.2 of the chapter, which identifies the educational goal, curriculum emphasis, and teaching methods for each of the educational philosophies.

53. Criteria for response:

   The response should state that forming a personal philosophy is important because it helps you explain and defend your educational goals—what you're trying to accomplish in the classroom. The response should then include an example (such as a teacher whose work is grounded in essentialism emphasizing testing because it helps students acquire essential knowledge).

CHAPTER SEVEN ANSWERS

1.	a	10.	b	19.	a	28.	a
2.	a	11.	c	20.	b	29.	c
3.	d	12.	d	21.	d	30.	d
4.	b	13.	c	22.	c	31.	d
5.	c	14.	b	23.	a	32.	b
6.	d	15.	b	24.	a	33.	d
7.	b	16.	c	25.	a		
8.	a	17.	d	26.	c		
9.	d	18.	a	27.	d		

34. c Duties such as scheduling, collecting student records from teachers, keeping master records for the school, and maintaining communication with district-level administrators and parents typically are carried out by a vice principal or assistant principal.

35. d Scheduling and coordinating the statewide assessment tests that all the students are required to take and providing a variety of information about course offerings and future options for students are typically duties performed by guidance counselors.

36. b Because of concerns about student drug use, teachers are forbidden from administering any form of medication.

37. b Maintaining student discipline is typically a duty performed by an assistant principal.

38. d Decisions about what content to teach and the order in which it will be taught describe curriculum organization.

39. c The ability to consider the perspectives of others reflects social development.

40. a The process of keeping a teacher with a group of students for more than a year to provide them with further nurturing is commonly called *looping*.

41. a The developmental characteristics of first graders make cooperative learning most challenging with them.

42. d The social development of fifth graders has advanced to the point that cooperative learning is less challenging than it is with younger children.

43. b Common planning periods for teacher teams and an emphasis on integrating curriculum is characteristic of middle schools.

44. c Academic focus, high collective efficacy on the part of teachers, and ongoing assessment are characteristics of an effective school.

45. a "Most of the teachers at Gilchrist believe that they can promote learning for all students regardless of their backgrounds, and the teachers take personal responsibility for ensuring that learning takes place" appears in the vignette, whereas Ridgeview teachers state, "In some cases, because of the background of the kids, we can't do a whole lot about their academics." The evidence indicates higher collective efficacy at Gilchrist than at Ridgeview.

46. d Interactive instruction (based on teacher questioning) is more effective than instruction based on teacher lecture and explaining.

47. b Research evidence indicates that high-SES students perform better than low-SES students in all schools, but the achievement gap is narrower when the collective efficacy is high.

48. Criteria for response:
    The response should state that a social institution is an organization with established structures and rules designed to promote certain goals. It should then argue that families do or do not have established structures and they either do or do not promote certain goals.

49. Criteria for response:
    The response should state that learner development, economics, and politics are the primary reasons for the way schools are organized. The response should then provide explanations (such as small children needing the security of a single teacher as a reason for having elementary schools self-contained).

50. Criteria for response:
    The response should state that the practice of placing students in different ability tracks and large size are two common criticisms of comprehensive high schools. The response should then include explanations (such as the generally lower quality of instruction and the disproportionate number of cultural minorities in low-level tracks).

51. Criteria for response:

The response should state that personal teaching efficacy is a teacher's belief in his or her ability to promote learning in all students regardless of their background or ability. It should then state that a school has high collective efficacy when most of the teachers are high in personal teaching efficacy. The response should also state that the concepts are important because, when present, they increase achievement for all learners and narrow the achievement gap between high and low achievers.

52. Criteria for response:

The response should state that student achievement is higher for all students in high-collective-efficacy schools, and the achievement gap between high- and low-SES students is narrower in these schools.

53. Criteria for response:

The response should include the information from Figure 7.1 of the chapter. It should then include an explanation for each (such as effective schools being neither too small nor too large as an explanation for the school-size characteristic of school organization and climate).

CHAPTER EIGHT ANSWERS

1.	c	11.	a	21.	d	31.	c
2.	d	12.	b	22.	a	32.	a
3.	b	13.	b	23.	a	33.	d
4.	b	14.	d	24.	d	34.	c
5.	a	15.	b	25.	c	35.	d
6.	d	16.	c	26.	c	36.	b
7.	b	17.	c	27.	c	37.	a
8.	c	18.	d	28.	c	38.	c
9.	b	19.	d	29.	c		
10.	d	20.	a	30.	b		

39. b   Local districts and schools are required to select textbook series from state-approved lists.

40. c   The trend in structuring school districts is toward fewer and larger districts. This is generally true in all areas of the country.

41. d   Local school boards are composed of lay people who are elected by the citizens of the district.

42. b   Policies that govern student attendance in local districts are established by local school boards.

43. a   Policies that govern student dress, participation in extracurricular activities, and all other aspects of school that affect students are established by local school boards.

44. c   The school principal is primarily responsible for hiring teachers for his or her school, so whether or not you get the job will be largely determined by the school principal.

45. d   Differences in school facilities are largely determined by a district's funding, which depends primarily on local property taxes.

46. d   Site-based decision making puts more of school governance in the hands of teachers and parents than exists in schools not committed to site-based decision making. As a result teachers in a school committed to site-based decision making will spend more of their time on governance issues, which will involve a considerable amount of committee work.

47. Criteria for response:

The response should state that small districts have the advantage of being less bureaucratic and easier to influence, but they have the disadvantage of not being able to provide as many resources and support services as large districts. Large districts have the advantage of being able to provide services, but they tend to be bureaucratic. The response should then explain each (such as an individual school being unable to acquire extra staff for students with exceptionalities because of the difficulty getting the request through the bureaucracy).

48. Criteria for response:

The response should identify making financial decisions, hiring and firing personnel, making curriculum decisions, establishing policies that affect students, and creating an infrastructure as the functions of school boards. The response should then include an example that explains each (such as setting attendance, dress, and behavior standards for students in the district as an example of policies that affect students).

49. Criteria for response:

The response should state that few cultural minorities serve on local school boards (about 15%), but the population they serve is about one third minorities, and local school board members tend to be wealthier than teachers. The response should then explain why these disparities are important (such as board members not being able to empathize with teachers who struggle to support a family on a teacher's salary).

50. Criteria for response:

The response should state that one disadvantage is the fact that the resources in different districts vary dramatically and that property taxes are politically unpopular. The response should then explain the disadvantages (such as a district in which many people own expensive homes collecting a great deal more money in property taxes than a district in which most of the people are lower SES, and property taxes being assessed once a year, making the amounts conspicuous, unlike sales taxes, which occur in small increments).

51. Criteria for response:

The response should state that sales taxes are regressive, meaning lower-income people pay a higher percentage of their income in sales taxes than do higher-income people. It should then include an explanation (such as a family of four that makes $25,000 per year spending about the same amount of money on food as a family of four that makes $75,000 per year, but the sales tax on the food being a much greater percentage of $25,000 than of $75,000).

52. Criteria for response:

The response should state that categorical grants are targeted for specific purposes, whereas block grants have few restrictions. It should then say that categorical grants have probably influenced education more than block grants because of their targeting specific groups (such as Title I programs that exist in schools and are funded by categorical grants).

53. Criteria for response:

The response should state that opponents of school choice argue that choice is likely to result in the polarization of enrollments and will further damage already weak inner-city schools. Proponents argue that schools are already polarized and cite statistics such as over half of all high school seniors being in classes composed of either more than 90 percent or less than 10 percent minorities. The response should then explain the positions (such as opponents arguing that when choice is allowed, better schools choose motivated students from affluent families, leaving less popular schools with lower-achieving, poorly motivated students.)

CHAPTER NINE ANSWERS

1.	b	8.	b	15.	a	22.	b
2.	a	9.	a	16.	b	23.	c
3.	b	10.	b	17.	d	24.	d
4.	d	11.	b	18.	b	25.	d
5.	c	12.	d	19.	d	26.	a
6.	a	13.	c	20.	b	27.	b
7.	d	14.	d	21.	c	28.	c

29. c   A well-defined personal philosophy can help guide your thinking. Supervisors and other teachers have no more legal or ethical guidance than you do.

30. d   The Civil Rights Act of 1964 is federal legislation. Each of the other answer choices is based on legislation from states.

31. c   Having a teaching license is a state requirement. Title I and the Individuals with Disabilities Education Act are pieces of federal legislation. A decision about your employment is made at the local level.

32. b   Requiring prospective teachers to take competency tests has generally been upheld by the courts.

33. c   Teacher contracts are legally binding for both parties.

34. d   Teachers are generally legally obligated to perform job-related nonteaching duties if the duties are connected to their teaching assignments (such as a physical education teacher being expected to coach).

35. c   In cases of overstaffing, first-year teachers can generally be dismissed or reassigned without a hearing.

36. c   In cases where teachers have been repeatedly warned and the teacher is using unconventional methods, dismissal decisions have generally been upheld in court.

37. d   Teachers' rights to include topics of their choice are generally upheld in court if the topics are related to the school curriculum and the teachers' goals and rationales for teaching the topics are clear.

38. c   The law is very specific in this case, and according to the law, you may copy the program and show it twice, but it must be erased within 45 days.

39. d   You are required to intervene whether or not they are your students and whether or not the incident occurs in your classroom.

40. d   If an allegation of child abuse is reported honestly and is based on evidence, teachers are protected from liability.

41. d   Teachers are legally responsible for being role models, and a DUI conviction could result in dismissal.

42. d   In court precedents teachers have been retained, and the court decisions have stated that the teachers' rights to employment outweigh the minor risk of infecting students.

43. c   Court decisions have stated that prayer is allowed if it is initiated by a student and doesn't interfere with other students or the functioning of the school.

44. b   In precedent-setting court cases religious study groups have been allowed to meet, with the courts concluding that schools must allow religious groups to use school facilities on the same basis as other extracurricular organizations.

45. a   In precedent-setting court cases, studying a piece of literature or other form of creative work has been allowed if the purpose in doing so is clear.

46. a   In precedent-setting court cases, the courts have ruled in favor of parents in situations identical to this one.

47. Criteria for response:
The response should state that laws are limited by the fact that they are written in general terms so they can be applied in a variety of specific situations, and they are written in response to past problems, so they may not apply to a present situation. The response should then include examples (such as the law not specifically stating what kinds of materials can be legally copied from the Internet and duplicated).

48. Criteria for response:
The response should state that codes of ethics are stated in general terms, which leaves them open to different interpretations. The response should then include an example to illustrate this limitation (such as the question of whether a teacher has "denied a student access to varying points of view" if the teacher takes a strong stand on a political issue).

49. Criteria for response:

The response should include five of the following: notification of the list of charges, adequate time to prepare a rebuttal, access to evidence and the names of witnesses, a hearing conducted before an impartial decision maker, the right to be represented by legal counsel, the opportunity to present counterevidence and cross-examine witnesses, a school board decision based on the findings in the hearing, a record of the hearing, and the right to appeal.

50. Criteria for response:

The response should state that copyright laws are federal laws designed to protect the intellectual property of authors. It should also state that fair-use guidelines allow teachers to make single copies of book chapters, magazine articles, and other materials for planning purposes, and short works can be copied for use in classrooms. It should also state that workbooks and other consumables may not be copied.

51. Criteria for response:

The response should state that in loco parentis is the principle the courts use to assess the limits of teacher responsibility, whereas negligence occurs when teachers fail to properly protect students from injury. The response should then explain or illustrate each (such as saying that the principle of in loco parentis means that teachers are required to use the same judgment and care that parents would use in protecting the children under their supervision).

52. Criteria for response:

Although the guidelines for teaching religious topics are often blurred, most commonly they suggest that teachers may teach *about* religious topics, such as the role of religion in the Crusades, but endorsing a particular religion or promoting a particular religious view is forbidden. Although difficult, teachers are expected to remain dispassionate with respect to religious topics.

53. Criteria for response:

The response should state that the FERPA provides for the following: informing parents of their rights regarding their child's records, providing parents access to their child's school records, maintaining procedures that allow parents to challenge and possibly amend information they believe to be inaccurate, and protecting parents from disclosure of confidential information to third parties without their consent. The response should also state that students' records are important because they can influence admission to special programs, acceptance to colleges, and employment.

54. Criteria for response:

The response should state that the following guidelines must be followed for states in which corporal punishment is legal (it is legal in 23 states): The punishment is intended to correct misbehavior; the punishment is administered without anger or malice; and the punishment isn't cruel or excessive and doesn't result in permanent injury. The response should also state that behavioral psychologists strongly discourage the use of corporal punishment because it communicates that force is a viable means of solving problems, which is precisely the opposite of the message schools want to send to students.

55. Criteria for response:

The response should state that students' due process rights include the following: a written notice specifying charges, a description of the procedures to be used, including the nature of evidence and names of witnesses, the right of students to cross-examine and present their own evidence, a written or taped record of the proceedings as well as the findings and recommendations, and the right of appeal. The response should also state that students' and teachers' due process rights are very similar.

CHAPTER TEN ANSWERS

1.	a	10.	d	19.	a	28.	c
2.	b	11.	b	20.	d	29.	c
3.	d	12.	a	21.	b	30.	c
4.	c	13.	c	22.	a	31.	c
5.	b	14.	d	23.	c	32.	b
6.	a	15.	d	24.	b	33.	a
7.	a	16.	d	25.	b	34.	d
8.	d	17.	c	26.	d		
9.	c	18.	a	27.	c		

35.   c   Goals and the reasons for the goals are decisions based on thinking about curriculum.

36.   b   Displaying two sample persuasive essays on the overhead, one that is well written and one that isn't, and guiding students' understanding in a discussion are decisions based on thinking about instruction.

37.   b   Wanting them "to learn that being uncertain is all a part of the learning process" is part of unstated aspects of the curriculum that students learn through the ways teachers interact with them.

38.   a   The specific topics she taught and the emphasis she put on them makes up the explicit curriculum.

39.   b   Anya's attitude and her emphasis on everyone having a right to speak are part of the implicit curriculum.

40.   d   The topics Anya didn't include make up the null curriculum.

41.   c   Rosano's attempt to integrate her science topics with language arts and her strong emphasis on language arts are typical of elementary schools.

42.   b   Curriculum integration and the fact that Janet and Joe are on the same team are evidence that they teach in a middle school.

43.   d   The fact that David teaches life science and that he doesn't know who Jeremy's English teacher is indicates that he teaches in a junior high.

44.   a   Geometry and chemistry are topics taught in high schools, and the fragmentation of the curriculum as indicated by the fact that Jeff didn't know what topics were being studied in other classes is characteristic of curriculum in high schools.

45.   a   Districts' rights to create a sex education curriculum have generally been held up in court, and parents who object have been allowed to remove their children from attendance.

46.   b   Wanting to teach some values, like honesty, and working on and reinforcing them are consistent with the views of character education.

47.   d   Wanting to have some "serious discussions with the kids" to help them understand their own values is consistent with the views of moral education.

48.   a   States' rights to require a service-learning component have generally been held up in court, based on the argument that service-learning courses promote citizenship and social responsibility.

49. Criteria for response:

The response should state that proponents of curriculum integration argue that it increases the relevance of content for students, improves achievement, and promotes collaborative planning. The response should also state that opponents argue that integrating curriculum results in a de-emphasis on some important concepts since teachers don't have a deep understanding of all the content areas that are to be integrated and planning and instruction for integrating curriculum are very time consuming. The response should also state that the results with respect to learning are uncertain, with some research suggesting that learning is increased and other research finding either no benefits or in some cases negative results.

50. Criteria for response:

The response should state that research indicates that participation in sports tends to decrease behavior problems and increase positive attitudes toward school. It should also state that girls who participate in sports have lower pregnancy rates, are less likely to be sexually active, and have fewer sexual partners.

51. Criteria for response:

The response should indicate that states influence curriculum by providing curriculum guides that include lists of objectives, creating state-mandated tests, and specifying graduation requirements. The response should then explain each aspect (such as saying that teachers will emphasize the content that will be measured on statewide assessment tests).

52. Criteria for response:

   The response should state that outcomes-based education attempts to describe curriculum in terms of objectives or results (outcomes). The response should also state that proponents argue that if we want students to acquire specific knowledge or skills, we should specify, teach, and test accordingly, whereas critics contend that many of the most important skills (like critical thinking) can't be specified explicitly, and trying to do so promotes minimal standards.

53. Criteria for response:

   The response should state that suggested reforms in all content areas propose moving away from having students memorize information and toward deeper understanding, putting students in active roles, and having teachers guide learner understanding. The response should then explain each reform (such as teachers guiding students' involvement in learning activities through skilled questioning instead of simply lecturing to students).

54. Criteria for response:

   The response should state that parental choice and control over children's education is one side of the issue, suggesting that parents should have a say in the books their children read. The response should also point out that professional autonomy is on the other side of the issue, asserting that teachers should be free to select books that they feel are important for student learning. Finally, the response should say that the courts have usually decided against censorship of books, ruling that schools have a right to expose students to different points of view through literature.

55. Criteria for response:

   The response should state that historically women and minorities have been underrepresented in the curriculum. It should then state that some critics charge that cultural minorities remain underrepresented in the curriculum, and the contributions of men of northern European descent are viewed as out of balance and irrelevant to cultural minorities. The response should then state that countercritics argue that too much emphasis on the contributions of minorities leads to racial and ethnic separatism and that we've already gone too far in emphasizing cultural differences. These critics also assert that we are all Americans and the increased emphasis on diversity has resulted in the failure of students to develop a shared national identity.

CHAPTER ELEVEN ANSWERS

1.	a	9.	d	17.	d	25.	a
2.	d	10.	d	18.	c	26.	c
3.	a	11.	c	19.	c	27.	b
4.	b	12.	c	20.	a	28.	c
5.	a	13.	d	21.	d	29.	d
6.	b	14.	b	22.	b	30.	c
7.	c	15.	d	23.	d		
8.	b	16.	a	24.	d		

31. d Understanding adjectives and adverbs is a form of conceptual knowledge, and being able to identify them in context indicates understanding.

32. a Believing that she can get Luiz to learn, regardless of the difficulty, is an indication of high personal teaching efficacy.

33. c Beginning classes on time is an indicator of being well organized. We don't have enough evidence to conclude that Karen is a more effective teacher than is Sally, and we have no evidence about Sally's caring or personal teaching efficacy.

34. d The elimination of vague terms describes the concept of language clarity, which is part of communication.

35. d Verbal statements indicating that one topic or idea is ending and another is beginning are transition signals.

36. b You explained (or directed Devon to explain) the reason for a rule against running, and you had him go back and walk through the hall, which is a logical consequence.

37. d Knowing what is going on in all parts of the room at all times illustrates teacher withitness.

38. c Knowing that you're a "dead duck" if you miss a homework assignment is an indicator of high expectations.

39. a The comment "I know all of you in here can understand this stuff if I teach it well enough" is an indicators of high personal teaching efficacy.

40. c In saying, "Now, keep that in mind because it's important," La-Juan was emphasizing the fact that electrons are sometimes fairly easy to scrape off atoms.

41. c La-Juan called on a different student for each of the questions she asked in this sequence.

42. d In these two paragraphs La-Juan used high-quality examples to illustrate her topic.

43. c When La-Juan rubbed the balloon and made Michelle's hair stick up, she was providing an example of static electricity.

44. d The questions in paragraphs 6, 11, and 14 required only recall of facts. The question in paragraph 8 required Kathleen to provide evidence for her conclusion.

45. d The appropriate level of question depends on the teacher's goal. All questions can be effective if they help students reach the goal.

46. b In paragraph 31 La-Juan provided Tracey with information about her answer. Providing information is the most important characteristic of effective feedback.

47. d La-Juan called on Tracey in paragraph 27, who was unable to answer (28). La-Juan then prompted her in paragraph 29, and Tracey was then able to answer (30).

48. d By having the students explain the additional examples, she was able to measure their understanding of static electricity.

49. Criteria for response:
    The response should state that both high- and low-level questions can be effective if they help students reach the teacher's goal. Helping students reach the goal is the basis teachers use for deciding what type of question to ask.

50. Criteria for response:
    The response should state that La-Juan's instruction was very well aligned. Her goal was for students to understand static electricity (paragraph 1), she provided examples that illustrated static electricity (paragraph 17), and she assessed their understanding with additional examples (paragraph 38).

51. Criteria for response:

The response should state that La-Juan's questioning was very effective. She called on a variety of students (paragraphs 6, 8, 11, 14, 17, etc.), she developed her lesson with questions, she paused to give students a chance to think, and all her questions pointed students to her goal.

52. Criteria for response:

The response should state that La-Juan effectively presented her subject matter. She showed concrete examples (her model in paragraph 6 and her demonstration with static electricity in paragraph 17), and she guided students to an understanding with her questioning.

53. Criteria for response:

The response should state that, for behaviorists, learning is a change in observable behavior occurring as the result of experience, and learning occurs when students give specific, observable responses to questions. The response should then include an example (such as a teacher saying, "Right!" when a student says "54" in response to the question, "What is 6 times 9?").

54. Criteria for response:

The response should state that learning from a cognitive point of view is a change in a person's mental representations of the world, which may or may not result in an immediate change in behavior. Learners try to make sense of what they experience and link it to what they already know. If the teacher's presentation doesn't make sense to them, they are likely to retain their existing ideas (such as clinging to the belief that bigger objects are more dense than smaller objects).

55. Criteria for response:

The response should state that teacher-centered means that teachers specify objectives, present the content to be learned, and actively direct learning activities, whereas learner-centered instruction involves teachers guiding learners toward an understanding of the topics they study, rather than simply explaining content to them. The response should then state that teacher-centered instruction has been criticized as being based on behaviorist views of learning and focusing primarily on low-level objectives at the expense of deep understanding. On the other hand, learner-centered instruction is criticized as being another example of "dumbing down" the curriculum, that learning basic skills is abandoned in favor of fuzzy thinking, and self-esteem is emphasized instead of understanding.

CHAPTER TWELVE ANSWERS

1.	a	10.	b	19.	c	28.	b
2.	a	11.	d	20.	c	29.	d
3.	d	12.	c	21.	a	30.	c
4.	c	13.	d	22.	d	31.	b
5.	c	14.	b	23.	b	32.	c
6.	b	15.	a	24.	c	33.	d
7.	a	16.	d	25.	d	34.	b
8.	a	17.	b	26.	a	35.	a
9.	b	18.	c	27.	d	36.	d

37. d   Having students use software to find melting points of various solids would provide data that could be used as background information for a lesson on physical properties of solids, so it would be used to support the teacher's instruction.

38. a   A tutorial that helps students learn to solve equations actually delivers the instruction. In each of the other choices, the technology is used to support the teacher's efforts.

39. b   Henry is working on basic math facts. Drill-and-practice programs can be effective for reaching fact-level goals.

40. c   The video clip allows the teacher to illustrate an idea that would have been very difficult to illustrate in any other way. This is characteristic of technology that supports instruction.

41. d   Drill-and-practice programs are effective for helping students reach fact-level goals.

42. d   The learning in this case involves more than memorizing basic facts. Tutorials can be effective for meeting these types of goals.

43. a   Simulations allow students to have virtual experiences without the disadvantage of—in this case—cutting up an actual frog.

44. d   The teacher linked written material, a simulation, and a DVD presentation. Linking different forms of technology in this way is using hypermedia.

45. d   Chatrooms involve e-mail communication among several people.

46. d   Learning and motivation goals are appropriate for utilizing technology. Putting students on the Internet without a clear goal, competing with other schools, and pleasing the principal are not.

47. b   Distance education involves linking people in learning situations through technology.

48. c   You presented the students with a problem—finding the relationships between natural resources and economies in different countries—and the students gathered information in an attempt to find these relationships. This is the essence of problem-based learning, which is an instructional strategy that uses a problem and the data gathered in attempts to solve it as the focal point of a lesson.

49. Criteria for response:

The response should say that the market economy and outmoded views of learning are the two primary factors. It should then explain by saying that companies are in the software business to make money, and quality is secondary to making a profit. The view of learning on which much software is based is an emphasis on drill-and-practice, which can reduce software programs to little more than electronic flashcards.

50. Criteria for response:

The response should say that computers can be used to (1) plan and construct tests (such as writing and storing items and printing tests), (2) score tests (such as machine scoring and summarizing results), and (3) maintain student records (such as keeping records on a spreadsheet).

51. Criteria for response:

The response should describe advantages such as Internet interactions being equitable and explain what equitable means by saying that factors such as attractiveness, prestige, and material possessions are eliminated. Internet communication can also be clearer because it gives students the time to form and present more complete thoughts, connect ideas, and think and reflect. The response should then identify disadvantages, such as Internet communication using only one channel, and explain that it uses only the written word, so students don't learn to read nonverbal social cues such as facial expressions and eye contact. Internet communication is also impersonal, leading to possible insensitivity and treating others like objects rather than people.

52. Criteria for response:

The response should state that some experts believe that schools have adequate access to computers (such as the research cited in the chapter saying that more than half of the nation's classrooms are connected to the Web and that schools have an average of one instructional computer for every 5.7 students). The response should also state that, on the other hand, many teachers believe access isn't adequate (such as 71% of teachers and 66% of principals saying an "insufficient number of computers" was a major obstacle to the use of technology).

53. Criteria for response:

The response should state that the advantages of labs include cost—it's less expensive to supply one lab with 30 computers than to buy 4 or 5 for every classroom in the school; a lab setting allows teachers to teach computer literacy skills in a whole-class format; and labs allow students to individually practice skills and receive feedback. The response should also state that classrooms have the advantage of allowing technology to be better integrated into the curriculum, but classrooms have the disadvantage of not having enough computers for all the students in the classroom, so organizing learning activities is an important issue.

54. Criteria for response:

The response should state that free speech advocates argue that access should be essentially unlimited and that Internet filtering is unconstitutional. It should state that critics counter that Internet filtering is no different from selecting curriculum content and textbooks for students, based on fundamental principles of good teaching.

55. Criteria for response:

The response should state that even high-quality software often doesn't match teachers' or districts' goals, so students often learn content that isn't related to what the teacher is trying to accomplish. It should also state that teachers report difficulties integrating technology into an already-crowded curriculum and that using high-quality software is even more time-consuming than using lower-quality software. The third part of the explanation should state that teachers already have too little time for preparation (less than an hour per day), and experimenting with and integrating technology into the curriculum create an additional planning burden.

CHAPTER THIRTEEN ANSWERS

1.	c	10.	c	19.	d	28.	d
2.	d	11.	d	20.	b	29.	c
3.	b	12.	b	21.	a	30.	b
4.	d	13.	b	22.	b	31.	a
5.	a	14.	a	23.	c	32.	d
6.	c	15.	d	24.	b	33.	d
7.	d	16.	c	25.	a	34.	a
8.	b	17.	b	26.	d	35.	c
9.	a	18.	a	27.	b		

36. b   Being able to create examples, such as Tim's vignette, requires both knowledge of content and pedagogical content knowledge.

37. c   Realizing that the book's presentation of the content was too abstract to make it meaningful to the students demonstrates Tim's knowledge of learners and learning.

38. c   Tim's classroom organization is an indicator of general pedagogical knowledge.

39. a   Tim demonstrated each of the four kinds of knowledge that effective teachers possess. This is an indicator of teaching expertise.

40. c   The description is taken from the INTASC standards.

41. d   Instructors react positively to students who are conscientious and who participate in class.

42. c   Instructors react negatively to students who aren't interested in learning for its own sake.

43. d   Instructors see through students' attempts to "suck up."

44. a   With respect to setting the professional tone, the principal is the most important individual in the school.

45. d   Organization is essential for first-year teachers because for them time is extremely scarce.

46. c   Research indicates that classroom management and effective instruction are interdependent.

47. b   Planning, knowing students' names, and questioning skills are essential for preventing management problems and teaching effectively.

48. Criteria for response:

The response should state that working conditions, dissatisfaction with student behavior, and loneliness and isolation are three commonly cited reasons that beginning teachers give for leaving the profession after their first year. It should then explain each (such as explaining working conditions by saying that teachers often spend too much time on nonteaching duties, have too little time for planning, and don't have a moment to themselves).

49. Criteria for response:

The response should state that beginning teachers commonly believe that the most effective way to help students understand a particular topic is to carefully explain the topic to them. This is most likely the result of their own experience; in most of their classes teachers have done little more than explain topics to them.

50. Criteria for response:

The response should state that proponents of alternative licensure claim that alternative teacher candidates are generally more capable than their traditional counterparts because they're older, they've had more life experiences, they're more focused on learning to teach, and they're more academically talented than are traditional undergraduates. Proponents also argue that because these programs are shorter, they can attract minorities and talented and experienced people in areas of critical need, such as math and science. The response should also state that critics counter that graduates of alternative licensure programs receive limited training in pedagogy; the intensive mentoring that is supposed to compensate for the lack of formal course-work rarely exists; alternative licensure graduates are disproportionately assigned to the most demanding teaching situations, such as inner-city schools; and they drop out of teaching at three times the rate of beginning teachers from traditional programs.

51. Criteria for response:

The response should identify (1) specifying a goal, (2) determining how your experiences relate to the goal, (3) strategically collecting items that provide evidence of your developing knowledge and skill, (4) deciding what items best illustrate your knowledge and skills, and (5) determining how to best present the items to the people connected to your goal. The response should then explain each step (such as saying that a video clip of you working with a student would be an effective entry as an example for step 4).

52. Criteria for response:

The response should state that electronic portfolios have the advantage of being more efficient than traditional portfolios and then should explain the advantage by saying that one CD-ROM would more than hold all the contents of a traditional portfolio. The response should then say that electronic portfolios have the disadvantage of requiring sophisticated technology that many people may not have.

53. Criteria for response:

The response should include four of the items from Table 13.3 of the text. Each of the items is described in the table.

54. Criteria for response:

The response should state that action research is a form of applied research that is designed to answer a specific school- or classroom-related question. It should also include the following steps: (1) identify and diagnose a problem that is important to you; (2) systematically plan and conduct a research study; (3) implement the findings to solve or improve a local problem; and (4) use the results of the study to generate additional research.